# MORE SLOW COOKER COOKER FAVOURITES

D0588626

10 9 8 7 6 5 4 3

BBC Books, an imprint of Ebury Publishing
20 Vauxhall Bridge Road,
London SW1V 2SA

BBC Books is part of the Penguin Random House
group of companies whose addresses can
be found at global.penguinrandomhouse.com

Penguin
Random House
UK

Photographs © BBC Magazines 2013
Recipes © BBC Magazines 2013
Book design © Woodlands Books Ltd 2013
All recipes contained in this book first
appeared in BBC *Good Food* magazine.

First published by BBC Books in 2013

www.eburypublishing.co.uk

A CIP catalogue record for this book
is available from the British Library

ISBN 9781849906708

Printed and bound in China by Toppan Leefung

Commissioning Editor: Muna Reyal
Project Editor: Lizzy Gaisford
Designer: Kathryn Gammon
Production: Rebecca Jones
Picture Researcher: Gabby Harrington
Cover Design: Interstate Creative Partners Ltd

## PICTURE CREDITS

BBC *Good Food* magazine and BBC Books
would like to thank the following people for
providing photos. While every effort has
been made to trace and acknowledge all
photographers, we should like to apologise
should there be any errors or omissions.

Peter Cassidy p95, p137, p165, p177, p205;
Jean Cazals p13, p61; Will Heap p69, p85,
p89, p111, p123, p203; David Loftus p161;
Gareth Morgans p87, p107; David Munns p6,
p23, p25, p27, p77, p79, p81, p83, p91, p101,
p109, p127, p149, p159, p173, p181; Myles New
p31, p33, p35, p41, p43, p51, p53, p59, p67, p73,
p75, p99, p115, p121, p129, p131, p147, p163, p167,
p169, p175, p185 p197, p207, p209, p211;
Stuart Ovenden p11, p15, p19, p37, p55, p57,
p93, p113, p39, p141, p145, p151, p185; Lis Parsons
p45, p63, p71, p103, p97, p125, p133, p143, p157
p195; Charlie Richards p17; Howard Shooter
p193; Maja Smend p21, p153, p155, p191, p199,
p201; Phillip Webb p29, p39, p47, p65, p119,
p135, p187, p189; John Whitaker p49, p117;
Kate Whitaker p105

All the recipes in this book were created
by the editorial team at *Good Food* and
by regular contributors to BBC Magazines.

# MORE SLOW COOKER FAVOURITES

EDITOR
Sarah Cook

BOOKS

# Contents

# Introduction

Our first slow cooker recipe book was such a success that we've created another! Packed with a further 101 inspiring recipes from the *Good Food* kitchen and plenty of clever tips and tricks, this new edition will really make sure you get the very best from the most helpful gadget on your worktop.

From a *Chicken, ham, leek & roast-potato pie* that is sure to become a family favourite to crowd-pleasing *Creamy tomato soup*, and even a *Cranberry jewelled mincemeat* you can gift to your friends at Christmas, like our first collection we'll show you just how versatile a slow cooker can be. This isn't just a book of stews and casseroles, but we have dedicated one special chapter solely to these, creating the recipes so they'll happily cook through the whole day – so no matter how hectic your life is, there can be a tasty hot meal ready and waiting for you when you get home.

There's a gorgeous section on effortless entertaining, too – who says a slow cooker recipe can't be glamorous? And there are plenty of puddings for those with a sweet tooth but little time on their hands to mess about. We've supper ideas that will have the kids asking for seconds, like our finger-licking-good *Stickiest-ever BBQ ribs*, and plenty of unusual ideas that will mean you'll never get stuck in a meal rut again – how does a yummy *Roasted-squash risotto with Wensleydale* sound for starters?

So whether you're a busy mum with hungry mouths to feed, a couple working long, tiring hours, or you just don't fancy standing by the stove pot-watching all evening, then this little book is perfect for you. What are you waiting for? Plug in the slow cooker and put your feet up – cooking has never been this easy!

*Sarah*

Sarah Cook

# Notes and conversion tables

## GETTING THE BEST FROM YOUR SLOW COOKER

Every slow cooker is different, so make sure you keep your manufacturer's manual handy when using it. However, here we'll share with you the *Good Food* team's top tips for slow cooking.

• Lots of the recipes can be changed to fit in with your lifestyle, so follow your manual's guidelines on decreasing or increasing cooking times by changing the temperature of the slow cooker. However, we've found rice and pasta dishes really work best when cooked on High for the shortest time possible.

• Always use easy-cook rice, if you can get it, and don't forget to rinse the rice well first. The more starch you can wash off the rice, the better the finished dish.

• Slow cookers vary considerably in size, so we've written a variety of recipes, for a variety of portions. Many of these are easily halved or doubled – check the individual recipes for recommendations.

• If the sauce of a stew or a casserole is a little thin for your liking, mix 1 tablespoon cornflour to a paste with a splash of the sauce, then transfer to a pan with a ladleful of the sauce and bring to the boil to thicken. Stir back into the stew and repeat if need be.

• If you want to adapt your own recipes to suit a slow cooker, look for something similar in this book and copy the timings – but reduce the liquid in your original recipe by around a third.

## NOTES ON THE RECIPES

• Eggs are large in the UK and Australia and extra large in America unless stated.

• Wash fresh produce before preparation.

• Recipes contain nutritional analyses for 'sugar', which means the total sugar content including all natural sugars.

SPOON MEASURES

Spoon measurements are level unless otherwise specified.

- 1 teaspoon (tsp) = 5ml
- 1 tablespoon (tbsp) = 15ml
- 1 Australian tablespoon = 20ml (cooks in Australia should measure 3 teaspoons where 1 tablespoon is specified in a recipe)

APPROXIMATE LIQUID CONVERSIONS

| metric | imperial | AUS | US |
|--------|----------|-----|-----|
| 50ml | 2fl oz | ¼ cup | ¼ cup |
| 125ml | 4fl oz | ½ cup | ½ cup |
| 175ml | 6fl oz | ¾ cup | ¾ cup |
| 225ml | 8fl oz | 1 cup | 1 cup |
| 300ml | 10fl oz/½ pint | ½ pint | 1¼ cups |
| 450ml | 16fl oz | 2 cups | 2 cups/1 pint |
| 600ml | 20fl oz/1 pint | 1 pint | 2½ cups |
| 1 litre | 35fl oz/1¾ pints | 1¾ pints | 1 quart |

APPROXIMATE WEIGHT CONVERSIONS

- All the recipes in this book list both imperial and metric measurements. Conversions are approximate and have been rounded up or down. Follow one set of measurements only; do not mix.
- Cup measurements, which are used in Australia and America, have not been listed here as they vary from ingredient to ingredient. Kitchen scales should be used to measure dry/solid ingredients.

*Good Food* is concerned about sustainable sourcing and animal welfare. Where possible, humanely reared meats, sustainably caught fish (see fishonline. org for further information from the Marine Conservation Society) and free-range chickens and eggs are used when recipes are originally tested.

# Curried squash, lentil & coconut soup

*Make for a weekend lunch, then save any leftovers for lunchboxes over the following week.*

**TAKES 4 HOURS ● SERVES 6**

1 tbsp olive oil
1 tbsp medium curry powder
1 butternut squash, peeled, deseeded
   and diced
200g/7oz carrots, diced
100g/4oz red split lentils
350ml/12fl oz vegetable stock
400ml reduced-fat coconut milk
chopped coriander leaves, to garnish
naan bread, to serve

**1** Heat the slow cooker if necessary. Mix the oil and curry powder to a paste in the slow cooker pot. Stir in the squash to coat, followed by the carrots, lentils, stock and coconut milk. Cover and cook on High for 3 hours until all the vegetables are tender.

**2** Using a stick blender or food processor, blitz the soup until it is as smooth as you like. Season and serve scattered with roughly chopped coriander and some naan bread alongside.

PER SERVING 178 kcals, protein 6g, carbs 22g, fat 7g, sat fat 5g, fibre 4g, sugar 9g, salt 0.4g

# Moroccan tomato & chickpea soup with couscous

*Ras-el-hanout contains cardamom, cinnamon, cloves, coriander, cumin, nutmeg, turmeric and pepper. Find it in larger supermarkets, or make your own mix.*

**TAKES 7–9 HOURS • SERVES 4**

3 tbsp olive oil

1 large onion, finely chopped

1 carrot, chopped into small cubes

4 garlic cloves, crushed

½ thumb-sized piece ginger, peeled and finely chopped

1–2 tbsp ras-el-hanout

1 tbsp harissa paste, plus extra to taste

400g can chopped tomatoes

500ml/18fl oz hot vegetable stock

75g/2½oz couscous

400g can chickpeas, drained and rinsed

juice ½ lemon

roughly chopped coriander, to garnish

**1** Heat the slow cooker if necessary. Put 2 tablespoons of the oil, the onion, carrot, garlic, ginger, ras-el-hanout, harissa, tomatoes and stock into the slow cooker pot, and give everything a good stir. Season, cover and cook on Low for 6–8 hours.

**2** Tip the couscous into a bowl, season with salt and pepper, and stir through the remaining oil. Pour over just enough hot water from the kettle to cover, then cover the bowl with cling film and set aside.

**3** Add the chickpeas to the soup then squeeze over the lemon juice. Cover and cook for 30 minutes on High, then taste and season. Uncover the couscous and fluff up with a fork. Spoon the soup into bowls, top each with a mound of couscous, scatter with coriander and serve with extra harissa for those who want it.

PER SERVING 265 kcals, protein 7g, carbs 33g, fat 10g, sat fat 1g, fibre 6g, sugar 10g, salt 1.2g

# Sort-of Scotch broth

*This broth is packed with barley, which makes it almost more stew than soup, so if you want it a little lighter, just halve the quantity of barley.*

**TAKES 5 HOURS • SERVES 6**

1 tbsp vegetable oil, plus a bit extra

750g/1lb 10oz lamb neck fillet, shoulder or other fatty stewing lamb, cut into generous chunks

1 onion, chopped

1 large carrot, roughly chopped

1 leek, chopped

1 celery stick, chopped

3 thyme sprigs

1 bay leaf

½ small white cabbage, roughly shredded

200g/7oz swede, diced the same size as the carrot

1.2 litres/2 pints vegetable stock

85g/3oz pearl barley

large handful parsley, chopped, to garnish

**1** Heat the oil in a flameproof casserole dish and brown the lamb – in batches if necessary – then remove to a plate with a slotted spoon. Add a drizzle more oil and tip in the onion, then soften for 5 minutes.

**2** Heat the slow cooker if necessary. Scrape the lamb and any resting juices into the slow cooker pot with the softened onions, the carrot, leek, celery, thyme, bay, cabbage and swede. Pour over the stock and season with a little salt and lots of pepper.

**3** Cover and cook on High for 3 hours. Then add the barley and cook for 1 hour more until the meat and barley are really tender and the vegetables are just starting to collapse. Scatter with parsley and ladle into bowls, adding a splash more hot stock if you want it more soup-like.

PER SERVING 388 kcals, protein 26g, carbs 22g, fat 22g, sat fat 9g, fibre 5g, sugar 9g, salt 0.7g

# Thai chicken soup

*This is perfect for a Monday night if you have a chicken carcass from your Sunday roast. Any leftover meat can be shredded and added with the noodles and veg.*

**TAKES 7–8 HOURS • SERVES 4**

140g/5oz soba or wholewheat noodles
100g/4oz beansprouts
2 pak choi, leaves separated
1 red chilli, deseeded and sliced
1 tbsp soy sauce
2 tbsp honey
juice 1 lime, plus extra wedges to
   squeeze over
4 spring onions, sliced, to garnish
½ small bunch mint, roughly chopped,
   to garnish

**FOR THE BROTH**

1 roasted chicken carcass
thumb-sized piece ginger, bashed and
   sliced
1 garlic clove, crushed
2 spring onions, sliced
5 peppercorns

**1** To make the broth, heat the slow cooker if necessary. Put the chicken carcass in the slow cooker pot. Just cover it with hot water, then add the rest of the ingredients, and cover and cook on Low for 6–7 hours.

**2** Strain the chicken broth into a clean pan. Carefully pick out any pieces of chicken and return them to the broth, but discard the bones. Put the broth back in the slow cooker pot.

**3** Add the noodles, beansprouts, pak choi, red chilli, soy sauce, honey and lime juice, adding the squeezed lime halves to the pot, too. Cook on High, covered, for 30 minutes more.

**4** Ladle the soup into bowls, scatter over the spring onions and mint leaves, and serve with the lime wedges for squeezing over.

PER SERVING 206 kcals, protein 15g, carbs 35g, fat 2g, sat fat none, fibre 2g, sugar 7g, salt 1.96g

# Chunky root vegetable soup with cheesy pesto toasts

*Try blending all, or half, of the soup for a different texture, and if you don't want to serve it with toasts, simply stir a spoon of bought pesto into each bowl.*

**TAKES 3½ HOURS ● SERVES 4**

25g/1oz butter
2 shallots, finely chopped
2 garlic cloves, crushed
100ml/3½fl oz white wine
1 medium leek, chopped
1 medium parsnip, diced
1 large carrot, diced
1 swede, diced
600ml/1 pint vegetable stock
100g/4oz mature Cheddar, grated
1 small ciabatta loaf, cut into 8 thin slices

**FOR THE PESTO**

25g pack each flat-leaf parsley and chives, finely chopped and snipped
25g/1oz Parmesan, finely grated
2 garlic cloves, crushed
a little olive oil

**1** Heat the slow cooker if necessary. Melt the butter in a small frying pan. Add the shallots and garlic, and cook for 5 minutes until soft, then pour in the wine and simmer until reduced.

**2** Scrape the shallots into the slow cooker pot. Add the leek, parsnip, carrot, swede and stock. Cover and cook on High for 3 hours until the vegetables are soft.

**3** Meanwhile, to make the pesto, mix all the ingredients together with enough olive oil to make a thickish paste. Season.

**4** To make the toasts, put the grated cheese in a bowl and mix together with 1 tablespoon of the pesto. Heat the grill. Put the ciabatta slices under the grill and toast them on both sides. Remove, top with the herby cheese mixture, then grill until melted.

**5** Season the soup well and serve with the cheesey pesto toasts and remaining pesto drizzled over.

---

PER SERVING 388 kcals, protein 15g, carbs 43g, fat 18g, sat fat 9g, fibre 9g, sugar 18g, salt 1.85g

# Courgette, potato & Cheddar soup

*This makes a big batch – perfect for using up a glut of cheap courgettes and potatoes, but if your slow cooker is small, simply halve the quantities of the ingredients.*

**TAKES 5 HOURS ● SERVES 8**

500g/1lb 2oz potatoes, unpeeled and
    roughly chopped
2 vegetable stock cubes
1kg/2lb 4oz courgettes, roughly
    chopped
bunch spring onions, sliced, save 1
    onion, thinly sliced, to garnish
100g/4oz extra mature Cheddar or
    vegetarian alternative, grated, plus
    a little extra to garnish
good grating fresh nutmeg

**1** Heat the slow cooker if necessary. Put the potatoes in the slow cooker pot with just enough water to cover them and crumble in the stock cubes. Cover and cook for 3 hours on High until the potatoes are tender.

**2** Scoop out a couple of ladlefuls of stock and save for the end. Add the courgettes and spring onions, put the lid back on and cook for 30 minutes more until the courgettes are tender.

**3** Take off the heat, then stir in the cheese and season with the nutmeg, salt and some black pepper. Whizz to a thick soup, adding the reserved stock until you get the consistency you like. Serve scattered with the extra grated Cheddar, spring onions and black pepper. Or cool and freeze in freezer bags or containers with good lids for up to 3 months.

PER SERVING 131 kcals, protein 7g, carbs 14g, fat 6g, sat fat 3g, fibre 2g, sugar 3g, salt 1.31g

# Hot & sour broth with prawns

*This makes a great starter before a Chinese meal; it's simple, but the key is allowing time to flavour the broth.*

**TAKES 2 HOURS, OR UP TO A DAY, IF YOU LIKE ● SERVES 4**

3 tbsp rice vinegar or white wine vinegar
500ml/18fl oz chicken stock
1 tbsp soy sauce
1–2 tbsp golden caster sugar
thumb-sized piece ginger, peeled and thinly sliced
1 lemongrass stalk, outer woody leaves removed and finely sliced
2 small hot red chillies, thinly sliced
3 spring onions, thinly sliced
300g/10oz small raw peeled prawns, from a sustainable source

**1** Heat the slow cooker if necessary. Put the vinegar, stock, soy sauce, sugar (start with 1 tablespoon and add the second at the end if you want the soup sweeter), ginger, lemongrass and chillies in the slow cooker pot. Cover and cook on High for 1 hour, or on Low for 4–8 hours, if you have time.
**2** When you're nearly ready to serve, add the spring onions and prawns. Cover and cook on High for 20–30 minutes until the prawns are just cooked.

PER SERVING 93 kcals, protein 17g, carbs 5g, fat 1g, sat fat none, fibre none, sugar 5g, salt 1.39g

# Caramelised-onion & barley soup with cheese croutons

*Pearl barley is deliciously nutty, nutritious and very cheap – a great way to bulk up soups and stews instead of using rice or pasta.*

**TAKES 3–4 HOURS ● SERVES 2**

1 tbsp olive oil

2 medium onions, thinly sliced

2 garlic cloves, thinly sliced

6 thyme sprigs, leaves chopped

1 tsp sugar

350ml/12fl oz vegetable stock

50g/2oz pearl barley, rinsed

60g/2½oz cavolo nero or kale, thick stalks discarded and leaves sliced

4 slices baguette, toasted

4 tbsp grated Gruyère

**1** Heat the slow cooker if necessary. Mix the oil, onions, garlic, thyme, sugar and a good pinch of salt in the slow cooker pot. Cover and cook on High for 2–3 hours, stirring occasionally, until the onions are very soft and caramelised.

**2** Add the stock, barley and cavolo nero or kale. Cover and cook on High for 30 minutes, or until the barley is tender.

**3** Heat the grill. Top the toasted bread with the cheese and put under the grill until it's bubbly and melted. Serve the soup in two large bowls with the cheesey croutons on top.

PER SERVING 419 kcals, protein 14g, carbs 57g, fat 14g, sat fat 5g, fibre 5g, sugar 12g, salt 1.2g

# Parsnip soup with parsley cream

*This gorgeous soup makes a great starter at a winter dinner party, with the extra-special touch of crispy fried-parsnip croutons and silky parsley cream.*

**TAKES 5, OR UP TO 9 HOURS**

● **SERVES 6**

1 onion, finely chopped

1 tbsp olive oil

700g/1lb 9oz parsnips, cut into chunks

3 bay leaves

300ml/½ pint whole milk, plus a drop
   more if necessary

300ml/½ pint vegetable stock

**FOR THE PARSLEY PURÉE AND CREAM**

2 × 80g packs curly parsley

150ml/¼ pint double cream

150ml/¼ pint whipping cream,
   whipped to soft peaks

**FOR THE GARNISH**

1 parsnip, cut into small cubes

1 tbsp olive oil

**1** Heat the slow cooker if necessary. Soften the onion in the oil. Transfer to the pot with the parsnips, bay leaves, milk and stock. Cover and cook on Low for 6–8 hours or on High for 3–4 hours until the parsnips are tender.

**2** Remove the bay leaves and drain parsnips, reserving the liquid. Whizz the parsnips in a blender, adding a little reserved liquid at a time until a good soup consistency.

**3** For the parsley purée, blanch the parsley in boiling water for 30 seconds, then refresh in iced water. Squeeze out any water, then whizz in a blender, with the double cream until smooth. Fold a little of the purée through the whipped cream. Season and chill.

**4** For the garnish, fry the parsnip cubes in the oil until golden and tender.

**5** Reheat the soup. Put the purée into six bowls, top with the soup, then the parsley cream and the parsnip cubes.

---

PER SERVING 393 kcals, protein 7g, carbs 25g, fat 30g, sat fat 15g, fibre 8g, sugar 15g, salt 0.32g

# Pea & watercress soup

*A perfect summer soup that you can adapt so you can serve it all year round. Use spring onions, rocket and sorrel in spring; frozen peas and leeks in winter.*

**TAKES 4 HOURS • SERVES 4**

1 tbsp olive oil

1 onion, finely chopped

1 garlic clove, roughly chopped

1 medium potato, cut into small chunks

700ml/1¼ pints vegetable stock

300g/10oz fresh peas (or frozen if out of season)

100g/4oz watercress

leaves from 2 mint sprigs, plus extra, chopped, to garnish

100ml/3½fl oz double cream

crusty bread, to serve

**1** Heat the slow cooker if necessary. Heat the oil in a frying pan, then gently fry the onion and garlic for 5 minutes or until soft. Scrape into the slow cooker pot with the potato and stock. Cover and cook on High for 2½ hours until the potato is almost cooked.

**2** Scatter in the peas and watercress, stir, cover, then cook for 20–30 minutes more until everything tender. Add the mint leaves and blitz with a stick blender until smooth. Stir in the cream and season to taste. Serve ladled into bowls, scattered with more mint and some cracked black pepper. Serve with crusty bread.

PER SERVING 256 kcals, protein 8g, carbs 17g, fat 18g, sat fat 8g, fibre 5g, sugar 5g, salt 0.21g

# Carrot, garlic & thyme soup

*This soup freezes well for up to 3 months, so if you have a large slow cooker, make a double batch.*

**TAKES 4 HOURS • SERVES 2, WITH LEFTOVERS**

small knob butter
2 onions, finely chopped
700g/1lb 9oz carrots, cut into batons
2 tbsp olive oil
4 garlic cloves, crushed
few thyme sprigs, plus extra to garnish
500ml/18fl oz chicken stock, made
    with 1 cube
6 tbsp double cream

**FOR THE CROUTONS**
6 slices pancetta
2 thick slices rustic bread, cut into
    soldiers (we used sourdough)
drizzle olive oil

**1** Heat the slow cooker if necessary. Put the butter and onions in a frying pan over a medium heat and cook gently until softened. Scrape into the slow cooker pot with the carrots, oil, garlic, thyme and stock. Cover and cook on High for 3 hours until the carrots are tender.

**2** Next, make the croutons. Heat oven to 200C/180C fan/gas 6. Wrap the pancetta around the bread soldiers, leaving the ends of the bread exposed. Put on a baking sheet, drizzle with a little oil and grind over some black pepper. Bake for 10 minutes until the pancetta and bread edges are crisp. Drain on kitchen paper.

**3** While the croutons are cooking, blitz the soup with a stick blender. Add 5 tablespoons of the cream and season. Serve drizzled with the remaining cream and garnished with thyme and the croutons scattered over.

PER SERVING 828 kcals, protein 28g, carbs 51g, fat 57g, sat fat 26g, fibre 12g, sugar 34g, salt 3.1g

# Spicy red-lentil soup with cheese chapatis

*This easy, warming soup uses cheap ingredients; so if you're on a budget this makes a great weeknight supper.*

**TAKES 4 HOURS • SERVES 4**

1 tbsp vegetable oil
1 onion, chopped
2 tsp cumin seeds
2 tbsp hot curry paste
250g/9oz red split lentils
1 litre/1¾ pints hot vegetable stock
4 chapatis
2 tbsp mango chutney
75g/2½oz mature Cheddar or
    vegetarian alternative, grated
2 spring onions, thinly sliced
juice ½ lemon

**1** Heat the slow cooker if necessary. Heat the oil in a large pan. Cook the onion and cumin seeds for 5 minutes until the onion is softened and golden.

**2** Tip the onions into the slow cooker pot and stir in the curry paste, followed by the lentils, and then the stock. Cover and cook on High for 3 hours until the lentils are tender. Whizz to smooth a bit in a blender if you like, adding a splash of hot water if it is too thick.

**3** Meanwhile, spread 2 of the chapatis with the mango chutney, sprinkle over the cheese and spring onions, then top with the remaining chapatis. Cook in a large non-stick frying pan, one sandwich at a time, for 3–4 minutes on each side until golden brown and the cheese is melting inside. Cut into wedges.

**4** Stir the lemon juice into the soup, and season if necessary. Ladle into four bowls and serve with a couple of the cheesey chapati wedges on the side.

PER SERVING 487 kcals, protein 25g, carbs 64g, fat 17g, sat fat 5g, fibre 4g, sugar 8g, salt 4.14g

# Walkers' wild mushroom, bacon & barley broth

*Dried porcini mushrooms give this soup a rich flavour, which the barley and veg soaks up. Do try it with a sprinkling of cheese – it lifts a bowl of soup into a meal in itself.*

**TAKES 8 HOURS • SERVES 6**

200g pack lardons, or rashers bacon, cut into small pieces
2 onions, chopped
2 garlic cloves, crushed
1 glass white wine
30g pack dried porcini or dried mixed wild mushrooms
4 medium carrots, chopped into small pieces
3 celery sticks, thinly sliced
1 sprig each rosemary and thyme
1 litre/1¾ pints chicken stock
100g/4oz pearl barley, well rinsed
½ small head spring greens or chunk Savoy cabbage, finely shredded
Small wedge parmesan or any strong hard cheese, grated, to sprinkle
crusty bread, to serve

**1** Sizzle the bacon for 10 minutes until golden. Add the onion and garlic, lower the heat and soften for 5 minutes. Tip in the wine, increase the heat and bring to a simmer.

**2** Meanwhile, put the mushrooms into a jug and fill up to the 400ml/14fl oz mark with boiling water. Soak for 10 minutes.

**3** Heat the slow cooker if necessary. Scrape the bacon mixture into the pot. Lift the mushrooms out of their juice with a slotted spoon and roughly chop. Add to the pot with the carrots, celery and herbs. Pour over the stock, plus the mushroom soaking liquid – avoiding the last few drops as they can be gritty. Cover and cook on Low for 5 hours. Add the barley and cook on Low for 1 hour.

**4** Add the greens or cabbage, and cook for 30 minutes on High (if the cabbage doesn't fit, boil it separately then stir in to serve). Season, then serve with cheese sprinkled over the top and crusty bread.

PER SERVING 264 kcals, protein 13g, carbs 26g, fat 9g, sat fat 3g, fibre 5g, sugar 9g, salt 1.6g

# Simple seafood chowder

*If you want to bulk out this soup or bump up your daily intake of veg, simply add a can of drained sweetcorn for the final 5 minutes of cooking.*

**TAKES 4½ HOURS • SERVES 4**

1 tbsp vegetable oil
1 large onion, chopped
100g/4oz streaky bacon, chopped
1 tbsp plain flour
400ml/14fl oz fish stock, made from
   1 fish stock cube
225g/8oz new potatoes, halved
pinch ground mace
pinch cayenne pepper
200ml/7fl oz whole milk
320g pack fish-pie mix (salmon,
   haddock and smoked haddock)
250g pack cooked mixed shellfish
4 tbsp single cream
small bunch parsley, chopped, to
   garnish
crusty bread, to serve

**1** Heat the slow cooker if necessary. Heat the oil in a frying pan over a medium heat, then add the onion and bacon. Cook for 8–10 minutes until the onion is soft and the bacon is cooked.

**2** Scrape the onion and bacon into your slow cooker pot and stir in the flour. Pour in the fish stock, add the potatoes, and cover and cook on High for 3 hours until the potatoes are cooked through.

**3** Add the mace, cayenne pepper and some seasoning, then stir in the milk. Tip the fish-pie mix and shellfish into the pot, and press down so it is just under the liquid. Cover and cook for another 20–30 minutes until the fish flakes easily when pressed.

**4** Add the cream, check the seasoning and sprinkle with the parsley. Serve with some crusty bread.

PER SERVING 422 kcals, protein 41g, carbs 21g, fat 19g, sat fat 6g, fibre 4g, sugar 9g, salt 2.3g

# Broccoli soup with goat's-cheese croutons

*This soup is smart enough to serve as a starter at a fancy dinner party, or if you prefer something more substantial for lunch, swap the croutons for a blue-cheese toastie.*

**TAKES 4 HOURS • SERVES 4**

1 onion, finely diced
1 tsp olive oil or knob butter
1 medium potato, finely diced
400g/14oz broccoli, head broken into
   florets and stalk thinly sliced
100g/4oz rocket leaves
700ml/1¼ pints vegetable stock
8 thin slices baguette
150g pack soft goat's cheese

**1** Fry the onion gently in the olive oil or butter for 5–10 minutes, until soft.

**2** Heat the slow cooker if necessary. Tip in the softened onions, then add the potato, vegetable stock and plenty of seasoning. Cover and cook on High for 1 hour, then add the broccoli, and cover and cook for 2 hours more until the potato and broccoli are tender.

**3** Stir in the rocket, cover and set aside for 10 minutes, then whizz the soup in a food processor, or use a stick blender, until smooth. Return to the pot and keep warm.

**4** Toast the baguette slices, spread each with a little goat's cheese, then grill if you like, or serve as they are with the soup.

PER SERVING 287 kcals, protein 16g, carbs 27g, fat 12g, sat fat 7g, fibre 6g, sugar 7g, salt 1.3g

# Chicken, lentil & sweetcorn chowder

*This creamy chowder is high in fibre due to the addition of lentils, but reassuringly low in fat.*

**TAKES 4 HOURS ● SERVES 4**

4 spring onions, trimmed and thinly sliced
450ml/¾ pint chicken stock
250g/9oz potatoes, diced
250g/9oz boneless skinless chicken breasts
300ml/½ pint skimmed milk
140g/5oz frozen or canned sweetcorn
410g can Puy lentils or green lentils, drained and rinsed
snipped chives, to garnish

**1** Heat the slow cooker if necessary. Put the spring onions in the pot with the stock, potatoes and chicken breasts. Cover and cook for 3 hours on High until the chicken and potatoes are tender and cooked through.

**2** Lift out the chicken breasts, ladle about a quarter of the soup mixture into a blender and whizz until smooth. Stir back into the pan with the milk, sweetcorn and lentils. Dice the chicken and stir it back into the soup.

**3** Cover and cook for 15–30 minutes more until hot through. Check the seasoning and serve in warm bowls, scattered with snipped chives.

---

PER SERVING 252 kcals, protein 31g, carbs 29g, fat 2g, sat fat 1g, fibre 6g, sugar 5g, salt 0.75g

# Creamy tomato soup

*This soup can be made all year round as it uses only canned tomatoes and passata. Make this for Bonfire Night and serve with plenty of cheesy bread rolls on the side.*

**TAKES 4 HOURS • SERVES 6**

1½ tbsp olive oil
1 onion, chopped
1 celery stick, chopped
140g/5oz carrots, chopped
250g/9oz potatoes, diced
2 bay leaves
2½ tbsp tomato purée
1 tbsp sugar, plus extra to taste
1 tbsp red or white wine vinegar
2 × 400g cans chopped tomatoes
250g/9oz passata
1 vegetable stock cube
200ml/7fl oz full-fat milk

**1** Heat the slow cooker if necessary. Put the oil and onion in a frying pan, and cook gently for 10–15 minutes until the onion is softened. Boil the kettle.

**2** Scrape the onion into the slow cooker pot with the celery, carrots, potatoes, bay leaves, tomato purée, sugar, vinegar, chopped tomatoes and passata. Crumble in the stock cube. Add 300ml/½ pint boiling water. Cover and cook on High for 3 hours until the potato is tender, then remove the bay leaves.

**3** Purée the soup with a stick blender (or ladle into a food processor in batches) until very smooth. Season to taste and add a pinch more sugar if it needs it. The soup can now be cooled and chilled for up to 2 days, or frozen for up to 3 months.

**4** To serve, reheat the soup, stirring in the milk until hot – try not to let it boil.

PER SERVING 148 kcals, protein 5g, carbs 21g, fat 5g, sat fat 1g, fibre 4g, sugar 14g, salt 0.9g

# Pineapple, fig & ginger chutney

*To sterilise your jars, wash them in very hot water and leave to drain. Once dry, put them in the oven at 160C/140C fan/gas 3 for 10 minutes before using.*

**TAKES 5–6 HOURS ● MAKES ABOUT 1.3KG/3LB**

1 large pineapple (about 1kg/2lb 4oz), or 400g/14oz prepared pineapple, roughly chopped

500g/1lb 2oz Bramley apples, peeled, cored and finely chopped

5cm/2in piece ginger, finely chopped

1 red onion, finely chopped

140g/5oz dried ready-to-eat figs, chopped

2 tsp black mustard seeds

½ tsp freshly grated nutmeg

200g/7oz light muscovado sugar

250ml/9fl oz cider vinegar

**1** Heat the slow cooker if necessary. Tip the pineapple into a food processor, then pulse until finely chopped. Tip into the slow cooker pot with the apples, ginger, onion, figs, spices, sugar and 2 teaspoons salt. Cover and cook for 2 hours on High until the apples are tender.

**2** Add the vinegar, cover and cook for another 2–3 hours on High until pulpy. Stir the chutney every now and then while it's cooking. Pot into warm sterilised jars, seal and label. Will keep for 3 months.

---

PER TBSP 44 kcals, protein none, carbs 11g, fat none, sat fat none, fibre 1g, sugar 11g, salt 0.21g

# Corn relish

*This is a great summer chutney served with hot dogs, burgers or pork chops. Make this when corn cobs are cheap, sweet and plentiful.*

**TAKES 3–4 HOURS • MAKES
350ML/12FL OZ**

1 tsp vegetable oil
1 shallot, finely chopped
200–250g/7–9oz fresh sweetcorn
(about 2 cobs)
1 red chilli, deseeded and finely
chopped
50ml/2fl oz cider vinegar
25g/1oz caster sugar
½ tsp dry mustard powder
handful coriander leaves, finely
chopped (optional)

**1** Heat the slow cooker if necessary. Mix all the ingredients in the pot – except the coriander, if using – along with ½ teaspoon salt. Cover and cook on High for 2 hours for a relish with a crunch, or for 3 hours if you want it softer.
**2** Add the coriander, if using, and leave to cool. Keeps for 1-2 weeks in the fridge in jars.

---

PER TBSP 24 kcals, protein 1g, carbs 4g, fat 1g, sat fat none, fibre none, sugar 2g, salt 0.18g

# Tomato & chilli harissa

*If you've grown more tomatoes and chillies than you can eat, turn them into this Middle Eastern spice paste. Use it in marinades, Moroccan tagines, dips and soups.*

**TAKES 4–5 HOURS ● MAKES 1 × 350G JAR**

1 tsp each caraway seeds and
   coriander seeds

½ tsp cumin seeds

100ml/4fl oz olive oil, plus a little extra

4 garlic cloves, peeled but kept whole

1 tsp smoked paprika

500g/1lb 2oz tomatoes, deseeded and
   chopped

3 red chillies, deseeded (use more
   chillies and leave the seeds in if you
   like it very fiery)

1 tsp rose water (optional)

**1** Heat the spice seeds in a dry pan until lightly toasted and aromatic, then lightly crush using a pestle and mortar.

**2** Heat the slow cooker if necessary. Mix the oil, garlic, toasted spices, paprika, tomatoes and chillies in the pot. Cover and cook on High for 2 hours until the tomatoes are softened and pulpy. Remove the lid and cook for 1–2 hours more, stirring occasionally, until tender and thickened.

**3** Remove from the heat, add the rose water (if using), then blitz with a stick blender or pulse in a food processor to make a rough paste. Spoon into a sterilised jar and pour a little oil on the surface to cover it completely. Will keep in the fridge for several months if you cover the surface with oil after each use.

PER TBSP 34 kcals, protein none, carbs 1g, fat 3g, sat fat 1g, fibre none, sugar 1g, salt none

# Traditional bread sauce

*Christmas just isn't Christmas without a good dollop of creamy bread sauce alongside your turkey.*

**TAKES 3½ HOURS • SERVES 8**

1 onion, studded with 6 cloves
200ml/7fl oz whole milk, plus an
    optional extra splash
3 tbsp double cream
6 black peppercorns
2 bay leaves, plus extra leaf to garnish
100g/4oz fresh white breadcrumbs
1 tbsp butter
freshly grated nutmeg, to season
thyme sprigs, to garnish

**1** Heat the slow cooker if necessary. Pop the onion in the slow cooker pan with the milk, cream, peppercorns, bay leaves and breadcrumbs. Cover and cook on Low for 3 hours until creamy, stirring very occasionally.

**2** Remove the onion and bay leaves, and add a splash more milk if you like your sauce thinner. Stir in the butter, season with salt, white pepper and nutmeg, then serve with a garnish of bay leaf and thyme sprigs. Alternatively, you can leave this to cool and chill, or freeze for up to 1 month until needed.

PER SERVING 124 kcals, protein 3g, carbs 12g, fat 8g, sat fat 4g, fibre none, sugar 2g, salt 0.31g

# Cranberry sauce

*If your slow cooker is big enough, make a double batch. This fruity sauce is great with ham, cheese and leftover-turkey sandwiches, of course!*

**TAKES 1¼ HOURS ● SERVES 8**

100g/4oz golden caster sugar
100ml/4fl oz orange juice
2 tbsp port
300g/10oz frozen or fresh cranberries

**1** Heat the slow cooker if necessary. Mix the sugar, juice, port and cranberries in the slow cooker pot. Cover and cook on High for 1 hour until the berries have popped but not completely collapsed.
**2** Turn off the slow cooker and uncover the pot and let the sauce cool and thicken slightly. Keeps in the fridge for a week, or freeze for up to 3 months.

PER SERVING 78 kcals, protein 2g, carbs 17g, fat 1g, sat fat none, fibre 2g, sugar 16g, salt none

# Homemade tomato sauce

*There's nothing quite like home made, and this posh tomato sauce will perk up bacon sandwiches, fish and chips and beefburgers.*

**TAKES 4–5 HOURS • MAKES 400ML/14FL OZ**

1 tbsp olive oil

2 onions, chopped

1 thumb-sized piece ginger, finely chopped or grated

2 garlic cloves, crushed

1 red chilli, deseeded and finely chopped

800g/1lb 12oz tomatoes, briefly whizzed in a food-processor or finely chopped

100g/4oz dark soft brown sugar

100ml/3½fl oz red wine vinegar

2 tbsp tomato purée

½ tsp coriander seeds

**1** Heat the slow cooker if necessary. Fry the oil and onions together until really soft. Tip into the slow cooker pot and add all the remaining ingredients. Cover and cook for 2 hours on High. Remove the lid and cook for 1–2 hours more, stirring occasionally until saucy.

**2** Cool slightly, then whizz in a blender or food-processor until smooth. If the sauce is a bit thick for your liking, stir in a dribble of boiling water. Push through a sieve, then funnel into a sterilised bottle or jar while still hot. Cool completely before serving. Will keep for 3 months in the fridge.

PER TBSP 28 kcals, protein none, carbs 6g, fat 1g, sat fat none, fibre 1g, sugar 6g, salt 0.02g

# Apple & sultana porridge

*If your slow cooker has a turn-on timer, you can prepare this the night before and wake to a gorgeous hot bowlful.*

**TAKES 2½ HOURS • SERVES 4**

100g/4oz porridge oats
500ml/18fl oz skimmed milk
4 apples, cored and diced
100g/4oz sultanas
1 tbsp soft brown sugar

**1** Heat the slow cooker if necessary. Put the oats and milk in the slow cooker pot. Stir in the apples and sultanas, then cover and cook on High for 2 hours.
**2** Give the porridge a good stir, add a drop more milk to loosen if you need. Ladle into bowls, sprinkle with sugar and eat immediately.

PER SERVING 256 kcals, protein 9g, carbs 47g, fat 2g, sat fat 1g, fibre 4g, sugar 34g, salt 0.2g

# Smoky bean, bacon & eggy-bread bake

*This is great for breakfast or brunch – make it when you have a gang staying for the weekend.*

**TAKES 10–11 HOURS • SERVES 6–8**

200g/7oz bacon lardons
½ tbsp sweet smoked paprika
1 tbsp red wine vinegar
1 tbsp dark muscovado sugar
2 tsp Worcestershire sauce
3 × 400g cans haricot beans, drained and rinsed
350g/12oz passata
5 eggs
125ml/4fl oz milk
10 slices white bread, crusts removed and halved to make triangles

**1** Heat the slow cooker if necessary. Fry the lardons to crisp up, then tip them into the slow cooker pot with the paprika, vinegar, sugar, Worcestershire sauce and the beans. Season and mix well. Cover and cook on Low overnight or for up to 9–10 hours.

**2** Tip the beans into an ovenproof dish and heat oven to 220C/200C fan/gas 7.

**3** Whisk the eggs and milk with some seasoning. Dip the bread triangles into the egg mix, then layer them over the surface of the beans. Pour the rest of the egg mix over the bread and cook for 20 minutes, or until the bread is puffed and golden.

PER SERVING (8) 418 kcals, protein 23g, carbs 46g, fat 16g, sat fat 5g, fibre 9g, sugar 11g, salt 2.5g

# Spinach-baked eggs with Parmesan & tomato toasts

*Baked eggs are simple to do and make a really good summery starter or light lunch for friends.*

**TAKES 1¼ HOURS • SERVES 4**

85g/3oz softened butter
3 tbsp grated Parmesan
6 shredded basil leaves
1 tbsp finely chopped sundried tomatoes
400g/14oz spinach leaves
4 eggs
8–12 slices French bread

**1** Mash together the butter, Parmesan, basil and sundried tomatoes, and chill.

**2** Wash the spinach and trim off any thick stalks. Put into a large pan, then cook, covered, for about 2–3 minutes or until the spinach is wilted. Drain well, pressing out all the excess water, then return to the pan with about a quarter of the butter mix, stirring until the spinach is glistening.

**3** Heat the slow cooker if necessary. Divide the spinach among four buttered ramekins, then break an egg into each. Season with salt and black pepper, then top with a slice of the butter mix. Sit in the base of a slow cooker, then pour in boiling water around the ramekins until half full. Cover and cook for 30–45 minutes on Low, until the eggs are to your liking.

**4** Meanwhile, grill the bread on one side until crisp, then spread the other side with the remaining butter and grill until crisp. Serve the eggs with the toast on the side.

PER SERVING 494 kcals, protein 20g, carbs 31g, fat 33g, sat fat 18g, fibre 4g, sugar 4g, salt 2.23g

# Lentil & lemon fettuccine

*This simple peasant-style dish is hugely satisfying and packed with protein. Use any pasta you fancy – spirals or shells work well, too.*

**TAKES 3½ HOURS ● SERVES 4**

140g/5oz Puy or brown lentils
50g/2oz butter, diced
1 medium onion, chopped
3 garlic cloves, chopped
zest and juice 1 lemon
300g/10oz fettuccine or linguine
150g tub Greek yogurt
large handful coriander, leaves and
    stems roughly chopped

**1** Heat the slow cooker if necessary. Rinse the lentils in a sieve and put in the slow cooker pot. Add the butter, onion, garlic and lemon juice and zest. Add 200ml/7fl oz water. Cover and cook on High for 3 hours or until the lentils are tender.

**2** When ready to serve, cook the pasta according to the pack instructions, then drain well and tip into the slow cooker pot with the Greek yogurt and coriander. Toss together, season and serve.

PER SERVING 511 kcals, protein 21g, carbs 76g, fat 16g, sat fat 9g, fibre 6g, sugar 6g, salt 0.28g

# Spiced-pumpkin pickle

*Delicious served with Indian food like spicy lamb chops or biryani. If your slow cooker is large, why not double the recipe and gift extra jars to friends?*

**TAKES 5 HOURS ● MAKES 2 JARS**

2 onions, chopped
thumb-sized piece ginger, finely
    chopped
1 green chilli, halved
2 tsp brown or black mustard seeds
1 tsp ground coriander
2 tsp turmeric powder
2 tbsp plain flour
200g/7oz caster sugar
200ml/7fl oz cider vinegar
750g/1lb 10oz chunk pumpkin, peeled
    and chopped into 2.5cm/1in pieces

**1** Heat the slow cooker if necessary. Stir the onions, ginger, chilli, spices, flour and sugar together in the slow cooker pot. Stir in the cider vinegar, then cover and cook on high for 2 Hours until the onions are soft.

**2** Stir in the pumpkin, cover and cook for another 1½ hours on High until the pumpkin is just tender. Take the lid off and cook for another hour until the liquid has reduced slightly.

**3** Divide between two hot, sterilised jars and cover. Cool completely. The pickle can be eaten straight away or left in the fridge, unopened, for up to 1 month.

---

PER TBSP 15 kcals, protein 1g, carbs 4g, fat 1g, sat fat none, fibre 1g, sugar 4g, salt trace

# Roasted-squash risotto with Wensleydale

*This risotto has a double hit of tasty butternut squash – a creamy, sweet purée cooked with the rice, and crispy roasted-squash chunks scattered over to finish.*

**TAKES 3½ HOURS • SERVES 4**

about 1kg/2lb 4oz peeled deseeded
    butternut squash, cubed
1 onion, chopped
1 garlic clove, crushed
25g/1oz butter
1 litre/1¾ pints hot vegetable stock
350g/12oz risotto rice
1 tbsp olive oil
handful pumpkin seeds
100g/4oz Wensleydale or vegetarian
    alternative, crumbled
small bunch chives, snipped

**1** Heat the slow cooker if necessary. Put half the squash, the onion, garlic, butter and 900ml/1½ pints of the stock in the slow cooker pot. Cover and cook on High for 2 hours until the squash is really tender. Mash the squash in the pot or whizz to a purée with a stick blender.

**2** Rinse the rice in a sieve until the water runs clear. Drain, then stir into the slow cooker. Cover and cook again on High for 1 hour until the rice is tender and creamy.

**3** Meanwhile heat oven to 200C/180C fan/gas 6. Toss the remaining squash in the oil in a roasting tin and roast for 15–20 minutes until tender and golden. With 4–5 minutes to go, toss the pumpkin seeds with a little salt, spread the seeds amongst the squash, then finish roasting.

**4** Season the risotto and loosen with the remaining stock if you need to. Serve in shallow bowls, scattering over the roasted squash and pumpkin seeds, crumbled cheese and chives.

PER SERVING 599 kcals, protein 17g, carbs 93g, fat 18g, sat fat 9g, fibre 8g, sugar 15g, salt 1.1g

# Pasta with creamy greens & lemon

*You can use whatever soft herbs you like in this dish. Chives, mint, parsley or dill all work nicely with the other flavours.*

**TAKES 1 HOUR • SERVES 4**

250g/9oz crème fraîche
250ml/9fl oz milk
zest and juice 1 lemon
85g/3oz grated Parmesan
2 garlic cloves, crushed
140g/5oz broccoli florets
100g/4oz frozen soya beans
100g/4oz frozen peas
100g/4oz mangetout
350g/12oz pasta shapes
handful basil leaves

**1** Heat the slow cooker if necessary. Whisk the crème fraîche, milk, lemon zest, Parmesan and garlic together in the slow cooker pot. Stir in the green vegetables and pasta shapes, then cover and cook on High for 30 minutes until the veg is just tender and the pasta is cooked.

**2** Stir in the lemon juice, some seasoning and the basil leaves and serve.

PER SERVING 734 kcals, protein 29g, carbs 75g, fat 36g, sat fat 22g, fibre 7g, sugar 9g, salt 0.5g

# Salmon, squash & prawn laksa

*A laksa is a flavour-packed coconut broth – you can add just about any seafood, noodles and Asian vegetables you like. This one pairs salmon with butternut squash.*

**TAKES 7–9 HOURS ● SERVES 6**

185g jar laksa paste (or use 2–3 tbsp Thai red curry paste)

1 small butternut squash (about 600g/1lb 5oz once peeled), cut into chunks

400ml can coconut milk

300ml/10fl oz chicken stock

140g/5oz medium rice noodles, soaked in boiling water and drained

300g pack beansprouts

400g/14oz skinless salmon fillet, cut into large chunks

200g/7oz tail-on raw prawns

bunch spring onions, sliced

small bunch coriander leaves and lime wedges, to garnish

**1** Heat the slow cooker if necessary. Mix the paste, squash, coconut milk and stock in the pot. Cover and cook on Low for 6–8 hours or until the squash is just about tender.

**2** Add the drained noodles, beansprouts, salmon and prawns. Cover and cook on High for 30 minutes until the fish is cooked through, but keep an eye on the fish through the lid to ensure it doesn't overcook.

**3** Stir through the spring onions, then sprinkle with coriander and serve with some lime wedges.

---

PER SERVING 445 kcals, protein 29g, carbs 34g, fat 23g, sat fat 11g, fibre 3g, sugar 9g, salt 1.18g

# Sweet & sour lentil dhal with grilled aubergines

*You could just make the dhal by itself for serving alongside a curry, but topping it with charred aubergine slices turns it into a great vegetarian meal.*

**TAKES ABOUT 4 HOURS, OR UP TO 8, IF YOU LIKE ● SERVES 4**

4 tbsp vegetable oil
2 medium onions, thinly sliced
2 garlic cloves, finely chopped
finger-length piece ginger, grated
2 tsp turmeric powder
1 tbsp curry powder
400g/14oz red split lentils, rinsed
2 tbsp tamarind paste
500ml/18fl oz vegetable stock
2 medium aubergines, cut into 2.5cm/1in slices
a few coriander leaves, to garnish (optional)
cooked basmati rice and mango chutney, to serve (optional)

**1** Heat the slow cooker if necessary. Meanwhile, heat 1 tablespoon of the oil in a frying pan and fry the onions, garlic, ginger, tumeric and curry powder until the onion has softened. Tip everything into the slow cooker pot and stir in the lentils, tamarind paste and stock. Cover and cook on High for 3–4 hours, or Low for 6–8 hours until the lentils are soft and mushy.

**2** Meanwhile, heat a griddle pan until very hot. Rub the remaining oil over the aubergine slices and season. Cook for 2–3 minutes each side until cooked through and charred. Eat with basmati rice, lime or mango chutney and a sprinkling of coriander, if you like.

PER SERVING 325 kcals, protein 15g, carbs 41g, fat 13g, sat fat 1g, fibre 7g, sugar 10g, salt 0.72g

# Pea risotto

*This risotto makes the most of peas by incorporating pea purée and pea shoots, as well as little sweet peas.*

**TAKES 1 HOUR 40 MINUTES** ●
**SERVES 4**

50g/2oz butter
1 onion, finely chopped
300g/10oz frozen or cooked fresh peas
1 litre/1¾ pints hot vegetable stock
350g/12oz risotto rice, rinsed until
    water runs clear
25g/1oz Parmesan or vegetarian
    alternative, grated
2 good handfuls pea shoots, to garnish
extra virgin olive oil, to drizzle (optional)

**1** Heat the slow cooker if necessary. Melt the butter in a frying pan, add the onion and gently soften for about 10 minutes until really soft. Meanwhile, put 100g/4oz of the peas into a food processor with a ladleful of stock and whizz until completely puréed.

**2** Put the onion into the slow cooker pot and stir in the rice and remaining stock. Cover and cook on High for 1 hour or until the rice is just tender and creamy.

**3** Stir in the puréed peas, remaining whole peas, Parmesan or vegetarian alternative and some seasoning, then turn off the heat, re-cover and leave to stand for a few minutes. Give the risotto a final stir, spoon into shallow bowls and top with some pea shoots and a drizzle of olive oil, if you like.

PER SERVING 503 kcals, protein 14g, carbs 80g, fat 14g, sat fat 8g, fibre 8g, sugar 6g, salt 1g

# Chicken, edamame & ginger pilaf

*Use an easy cook variety of rice as it's less starchy than regular varieties and will give you a better result – that's also why rinsing it thoroughly is important.*

**TAKES 1½ HOURS • SERVES 4**

2 tbsp vegetable oil
1 onion, thinly sliced
thumb-sized piece ginger, grated
250g/9oz easy cook basmati rice
1 red chilli, deseeded and finely sliced
3 boneless skinless chicken breasts,
  cut into bite-sized pieces
500ml/18fl oz hot vegetable stock,
  made with boiling water from a
  kettle
100g/4oz frozen edamame/soya beans,
  left at room temperature to defrost
coriander leaves and fat-free Greek
  yogurt, to garnish (optional)

**1** Heat the slow cooker if necessary. Heat the oil in a frying pan and soften the onion and ginger together. Put the rice in a sieve and rinse until the water runs clear.

**2** Put the rice into the slow cooker pot with the softened onion and ginger, the chilli, chicken and 400ml/14fl oz of the stock. Stir well, cover and cook on High for 1 hour until the rice is tender and the liquid absorbed – check the rice halfway through as you may need to add another 50–100ml/2–3½fl oz of the stock if it looks a little dry.

**3** Stir in the edamame/soya beans, re-cover, but turn off the heat. Leave for 5 minutes to heat through. Season to taste, then sprinkle with coriander and serve with a dollop of Greek yogurt, if you like.

---

PER SERVING 436 kcals, protein 32g, carbs 52g, fat 9g, sat fat 1g, fibre 3g, sugar 4g, salt 0.5g

# Quick chilli with creamy chive-crushed potatoes

*Using sausages instead of mince is a great cheat to add flavour without having to use lots of extra ingredients.*

**TAKES 4 HOURS, OR UP TO 8, IF YOU LIKE • SERVES 4**

454g pack reduced-fat pork sausages
2 tsp vegetable oil
2 red peppers, deseeded and sliced
2 garlic cloves, crushed
1 tsp each ground coriander, chilli powder and ground cumin
2 tsp caster sugar
2 × 400g cans chopped tomatoes with herbs
400g can red kidney beans in water, drained and rinsed
1kg/2lb 2oz new potatoes, skins on, thickly sliced
5 tbsp fat-free Greek yogurt, plus extra dollop to garnish (optional)
20g pack chives, snipped (optional)

**1** Heat the slow cooker if necessary. Squeeze three balls of meat from each sausage, then fry in a pan with the oil for 5 minutes until golden. Add to the slow cooker pot with the peppers, garlic, spices and sugar. Drain one of the cans of tomatoes, then tip the chunks into the pot with the second whole can of chopped tomatoes. Stir well, then cover and cook for 6–7 hours on Low or 3 hours on High.

**2** Stir in the beans and some seasoning, and cook on High for 30 minutes more, covered, to heat through.

**3** Meanwhile, put the potatoes in a large pan and boil for 10 minutes until tender. Drain the potatoes, then crush with a masher. Fold through the yogurt and chives, if using, loosen with a splash of water, then serve with the chilli. Top with a dollop more yogurt and sprinkling of chives, if you like.

PER SERVING 547 kcals, protein 31g, carbs 80g, fat 14g, sat fat 4g, fibre 11g, sugar 19g, salt 1.84g

# Stickiest-ever BBQ ribs

*Is there anything nicer than sticky ribs? We think so – ribs cooked in a slow cooker so they are meltingly tender and falling off the bone, then simply crisped up to serve.*

**TAKES ABOUT 8 HOURS,
PLUS MARINATING • SERVES 4 (OR 8
WITH OTHER BBQ FOOD)**

2 racks baby back pork ribs
2 × 330ml cans cola
2 tsp toasted sesame seeds (optional)

**FOR THE SAUCE**

8 tbsp tomato ketchup
8 tbsp brown sugar
2 tbsp soy sauce
2 tbsp Worcestershire sauce
2 tbsp sweet chilli sauce
1 tsp paprika

**1** Heat the slow cooker if necessary. Cut the ribs into small racks so they fit into your slow cooker pot. Pour over the cola and enough water to cover the ribs, then cover and cook on High for 5–7 hours, until they are tender but not falling apart.
**2** Meanwhile, put the sauce ingredients in a small pan. Gently heat, then bubble for about 2 minutes, stirring.
**3** When the ribs are done, carefully lift each on to kitchen paper to dry. Transfer to a roasting tin and coat with the sauce. Cover and chill for 1-24 hours to marinate.
**4** Heat the barbecue, or heat oven to 220C/200C fan/gas 7. Add the ribs (in the roasting tin, if using the oven) and cook for 20 minutes, turning occasionally, and basting often with the remaining sauce. When the ribs are hot through and crisping on the outside, slice to serve. Scatter with sesame seeds, if you like, and serve with any remaining sauce.

PER SERVING (8) 450 kcals, protein 25g, carbs 37g, fat 23g, sat fat 9g, fibre none, sugar 35g, salt 2g

# Summer vegetable curry

*Whether you're a vegetarian or not, you'll love this veg-packed low-fat curry. Just add rice, naan or poppadoms and lots of mango chutney.*

**TAKES UP TO 9 HOURS • SERVES 4**

1–2 tbsp Thai red curry paste
   (depending on taste)
2 onions, chopped
200ml/7fl oz vegetable stock
1 aubergine, diced
75g/2½oz red split lentils
2 red or yellow peppers, deseeded and
   cut into wedges
200ml can reduced-fat coconut milk
140g/5oz frozen peas
50g bag baby leaf spinach, roughly
   chopped
brown basmati rice, naan or
   poppadoms and mango chutney,
   to serve

**1** Heat the slow cooker if necessary. Mix the curry paste and onions together in the pot, then stir in the stock, aubergine, lentils and peppers. Cover and cook on Low for 6–8 hours until the aubergine is nice and tender.

**2** Add the coconut milk and peas, cover and cook for 30 minutes more on High. Taste for seasoning, then take off the heat and stir in the spinach. Cover again and set aside for 4 minutes to wilt. Serve the curry with rice, naan or poppadoms and mango chutney.

PER SERVING 171 kcals, protein 8g, carbs 20g, fat 6g, sat fat 3g, fibre 7g, sugar 12g, salt 5g

# Lentil ragout

*This sauce is also great spooned over jacket potatoes, or into halved peppers then topped with grated Cheddar and baked in the oven.*

**TAKES 8–9 HOURS • SERVES 6**

3 tbsp olive oil
2 onions, finely chopped
3 carrots, finely chopped
3 celery sticks, finely chopped
3 garlic cloves, crushed
2 × 400g cans chopped tomatoes
2 tbsp tomato purée
2 tsp each dried oregano and thyme
3 bay leaves
500g bag dried red lentils
500ml/18fl oz vegetable stock
500g/1lb 2oz spaghetti
Parmesan, grated, to garnish

**1** Heat the slow cooker if necessary. Mix the oil, onions, carrots, celery, garlic, chopped tomatoes, purée and herbs in the slow cooker pot. Cover and cook on Low for 6–7 hours.

**2** Stir in the lentils and stock, and cook on High for 1–2 hours until the lentils are tender. Season.

**3** If eating straight away, keep on a low heat while you cook the spaghetti, according to the pack instructions. Drain well, divide among pasta bowls or plates, spoon the sauce over the top and grate over some cheese. Alternatively, cool the sauce and chill for up to 3 days or freeze it in portions for up to 3 months. Simply defrost overnight at room temperature, then reheat gently to serve.

PER SERVING 662 kcals, protein 33g, carbs 120g, fat 9g, sat fat 1g, fibre 10g, sugar 14g, salt 1.05g

# Chicken, ham, leek & roast-potato pie

*Leave the pie filling cooking during the day, then come dinner time you just have to top it with pastry and finish it off in the oven.*

**TAKES 7½ HOURS • SERVES 4 WITH LEFTOVERS**

400g/14oz boneless skinless chicken breasts

140g/5oz thick-sliced ham, roughly chopped

450g/1lb potatoes, peeled and cut into big chunks

2 leeks, trimmed and sliced

2 tbsp olive oil

1 heaped tbsp plain flour, plus extra for dusting

400ml/14fl oz chicken stock

3 heaped tbsp crème fraîche

375g pack ready rolled shortcrust pastry

beaten egg, to glaze

**1** Heat the slow cooker if necessary. Put the chicken breasts, ham, potatoes and leeks into the pot. Drizzle over the oil, stir to coat, then sprinkle over the flour and mix well. Remove the chicken, press the vegetables and ham into a layer at the bottom, sit the breasts back on top and pour over the stock.

**2** Cover and cook on Low for 6 hours until the chicken is tender and cooked through. Fish out the breasts and cut into chunks, then tip everything into an ovenproof pie dish and stir in the crème fraîche and some seasoning.

**3** Unroll the pastry and roll a bit more to fit the dish. Put on top of the pie, trim the excess, use a fork to crimp the edges then press the pastry to the edge of the dish. Make a small hole in the centre.

**4** Heat oven to 200C/180C fan/gas 6. Brush with egg to glaze (making sure the steam hole isn't sealed). Cook for 30–40 minutes, until golden and hot through.

PER SERVING 920 kcals, protein 46g, carbs 76g, fat 48g, sat fat 15g, fibre 5g, sugar 3g, salt 2.3g

# Light chicken korma

*This curry is low-fat and low-calorie, so there's no excuse not to make it right away and tuck in!*

**TAKES 4 HOURS • SERVES 4**

1 onion, chopped
2 garlic cloves, roughly chopped
thumb-sized piece ginger, roughly chopped
4 tbsp korma paste
50g/2oz ground almonds
4 tbsp sultanas
250ml/9fl oz chicken stock
¼ tsp golden caster sugar
4 boneless skinless chicken breasts
150g pot fat-free Greek yogurt
small bunch coriander, chopped
few flaked almonds, to scatter (optional)
basmati rice, to serve

**1** Heat the slow cooker if necessary. Put the onion, garlic and ginger in a food processor and whizz to a paste. Scrape the paste into the slow cooker pot and mix with the korma paste, ground almonds, sultanas, chicken stock and sugar. Push in the chicken breasts, cover and cook on High for 2 hours until the chicken is cooked through and tender.
**2** Fish out the chicken breasts and dice into chunks. Stir back into the sauce. Cover and cook for 20–30 minutes more on High, just to heat through.
**3** Remove from the heat, stir in the yogurt and some seasoning, then scatter over the coriander and flaked almonds, if using. Serve with brown or white basmati rice.

PER SERVING 376 kcals, protein 40g, carbs 28g, fat 11g, sat fat 1g, fibre 3g, sugar 26g, salt 1.1g

# Bacon Bolognese

*Some children simply don't like mince, so this is a great version of the traditional Bolognese sauce that all the family can enjoy together.*

**TAKES 7–8 HOURS • SERVES 4**

200g pack smoked bacon lardons
1 tsp olive oil
2 large carrots, finely diced
3 celery sticks, finely diced
1 onion, finely chopped
190g jar sundried tomato pesto
200ml/7fl oz vegetable stock
400g/14oz spaghetti
8–12 basil leaves, shredded

**1** Heat the slow cooker if necessary. Fry the bacon in a pan with the oil until crisp, then tip into the slow cooker pot with the carrots, celery and onion. Stir in the pesto and stock then cover, and cook on Low for 6–7 hours until the veg has softened.

**2** Cook the spaghetti according to the pack instructions then drain well. Stir into the sauce with the basil and serve.

---

PER SERVING 694 kcals, protein 24g, carbs 81g, fat 31g, sat fat 7g, fibre 7g, sugar 11g, salt 2.1g

# Tomato & onion bake with goat's cheese

*This dish sounds simple but is really delicious. Serve with fresh crusty bread for mopping up all the lovely sauce.*

**TAKES 8½ HOURS • SERVES 4**

6 onions, halved (keep root intact)
4 garlic cloves, crushed
2 tbsp olive oil
680ml bottle passata
1 tsp sugar
85g/3oz white breadcrumbs
125g log goat's cheese, crumbled

**1** Heat the slow cooker if necessary. Put the onions in the slow cooker pot, cut-side down. Mix together the garlic, oil, passata, sugar and some seasoning, and pour over the onions. Cover and cook on Low for 8 hours, or until the onions are tender.

**2** Heat a grill and transfer the onions and tomato sauce to a baking dish, if you need to. Sprinkle over the breadcrumbs and goat's cheese, then grill until bubbling and golden.

---

PER SERVING 346 kcals, protein 14g, carbs 39g, fat 15g, sat fat 6g, fibre 5g, sugar 19g, salt 1.1g

# No-fuss shepherd's pie

*If you want to sneak in some extra vegetables, add a couple of sticks of diced celery with the carrots, and before you top it with mash, stir in a handful of peas.*

**TAKES 6–9 HOURS, DEPENDING ON WHAT YOU PREFER • SERVES 4**

1 tbsp sunflower oil
500g pack minced lamb
1 large onion, chopped
2–3 medium carrots, chopped
2 tbsp tomato purée
large splash Worcestershire sauce
350ml/12fl oz beef stock
900g/2lb potatoes, cut into chunks
85g/3oz butter
3 tbsp milk

**1** Heat the slow cooker if necessary. Heat the oil in a frying pan, crumble in the lamb and brown the meat, tipping off any excess fat – you may need to do this in batches. Tip the meat into the slow cooker pot with the onion, carrots, tomato purée, Worcestershire sauce and stock. Cover and cook on High for 4–5 hours, or Low for 6–8 until the meat is nice and tender.

**2** Heat oven to 180C/160C fan/gas 4, then make the mash. Boil the potatoes in salted water for 10–15 minutes until tender. Drain, then mash with the butter and milk.

**3** Put the mince into an ovenproof dish, top with the mash and ruffle with a fork. The pie can now be chilled and frozen for up to a month, or bake for 20–25 minutes until the top is starting to colour and the mince is bubbling through at the edges. Leave to stand for 5 minutes before serving.

PER SERVING 663 kcals, protein 33g, carbs 49g, fat 39g, sat fat 20g, fibre 5g, sugar 10g, salt 1.35g

# Turkey chilli & rice tacos

*Turkey mince is a good low-fat alternative to beef mince and is still rich in iron.*

**TAKES 3–4 HOURS • SERVES 4**

2 tbsp chipotle paste
400g/14oz pack turkey mince
100g/4oz easy cook long grain rice
400ml/14fl oz chicken stock
420g can kidney beans in water,
    drained and rinsed
140g/5oz frozen sweetcorn, defrosted
small bunch coriander, chopped
8 taco shells
½ iceberg lettuce, shredded
150ml pot soured cream
grated cheese and guacamole, to serve

**1** Heat the slow cooker if necessary. Heat the paste in a frying pan. When hot, add the mince and cook until browned, breaking it up well with a fork.

**2** Rinse the rice in a sieve until the water runs clear. Tip into the slow cooker pot with the mince and stock. Cover and cook on High for 2–3 hours until the rice is cooked.

**3** Stir in the beans and sweetcorn, cover and heat through for 20–30 minutes. Season and scatter over the coriander. Heat the taco shells according to the pack instructions, then serve with the mince mixture, lettuce and soured cream. Let everyone build their own dinner, adding grated cheese and guacamole.

PER SERVING 503 kcals, protein 38g, carbs 56g, fat 16g, sat fat 5g, fibre 7g, sugar 7g, salt 1.16g

# Chicken & broad-bean tagliatelle

*This creamy pasta sauce is light but definitely not lacking in flavour. Perfect for making in the slow cooker during summer when you'd rather be outside than in the kitchen.*

**TAKES 2½ HOURS • SERVES 4**

1 tsp olive oil
4 boneless skinless chicken breasts
175g/6oz frozen broad beans
85g/3oz double cream
6 tbsp Parmesan, finely grated, plus
    extra to garnish
150ml/¼ pint chicken stock
300g/10oz tagliatelle
juice 1 lemon
small handful flat-leaf parsley, chopped

**1** Heat the slow cooker if necessary. Heat the oil in a frying pan and brown the chicken breasts on both sides. Put in the slow cooker pot with the beans, double cream, Parmesan and chicken stock. Cover and cook on Low for 2 hours until the chicken is cooked through.

**2** Cook the pasta following the pack instructions. Shred the cooked chicken breasts and put into the sauce with the lemon juice and seasoning. Drain the pasta and stir into the sauce with the parsley. Serve sprinkled with more Parmesan.

PER SERVING 646 kcals, protein 52g, carbs 60g, fat 22g, sat fat 12g, fibre 5g, sugar 3g, salt 0.7g

# Beef cannelloni

*This makes a really nice change to lasagne, and it's a lot easier for little kids to manage. Make this big batch and freeze it in portions for up to 3 months.*

**TAKES 7–10 HOURS, DEPENDING ON WHAT YOU PREFER • SERVES 12**

1kg/2lb 4oz lean minced beef
1 tbsp olive oil
1 large onion, finely chopped
4 garlic cloves, crushed
1½ × 660g jars passata with basil
large pinch caster sugar
400g/14oz cannelloni tubes

**FOR THE TOPPING**

50g/2oz butter
50g/2oz plain flour
600ml/1 pint whole milk
140g/5oz soft cheese with garlic and
  herbs
140g/5oz Parmesan, grated

**1** Heat the slow cooker if necessary. Fry the beef in the pan with the oil until browned, breaking up the mince with a wooden spoon. Tip into the slow cooker with the onion, garlic, 1 jar of the passata and sugar. Cover and cook on High for 4–5 hours or Low for 6–8 until the meat is nice and tender.

**2** Make the white sauce. Heat the butter in a small pan. When melted, stir in the flour for 1 minute. Stir in the milk gradually to achieve a lump-free sauce, then bubble for 2 minutes while stirring. Remove from the heat and stir in the soft cheese with some seasoning.

**3** Heat oven to 200C/180C fan/gas 6. To assemble, pour the remaining passata into the base of two or three large baking dishes. Spoon the beef into the cannelloni tubes using a teaspoon and lay them on top of the sauce. Pour over the white sauce, then sprinkle with Parmesan. Cook for 40–45 minutes until the pasta is tender and topping golden.

PER SERVING 479 kcals, protein 31g, carbs 39g, fat 23g, sat fat 12g, fibre 2g, sugar 9g, salt 1.28g

# Veg & cheesey rice bake

*This is a great midweek supper that kids will love. It's a satisfying summer dish – particularly if you're a keen gardener and have a glut of crops to use up!*

**TAKES 7½–8½ HOURS • SERVES 4**

1 onion, chopped

1 tbsp olive oil

2 courgettes, sliced

1 aubergine, diced

450g/1lb fresh tomatoes, chopped (or 400g can chopped tomatoes)

200g/7oz risotto rice

2 eggs

140g/5oz Cheddar, grated

**1** Heat the slow cooker if necessary. Mix the onion, oil, courgettes, aubergine and tomatoes in the pot. Cover and cook on Low for 6–8 hours until the aubergine is tender.

**2** Heat oven to 200C/180C fan/gas 6. Cook the rice in a large pot of salted boiling water for 20 minutes, or until tender. Drain and mix with the eggs and two-thirds of the cheese.

**3** Transfer the vegetable mix to an ovenproof dish. Spoon over the rice mixture and smooth out. Sprinkle over the rest of the cheese and bake for 30 minutes until bubbling and golden.

PER SERVING 443 kcals, protein 20g, carbs 48g, fat 19g, sat fat 9g, fibre 6g, sugar 8g, salt 0.8g

# Boiled bacon with cabbage & carrots

*If you can't squeeze all the vegetables into your slow cooker then simply boil them separately and moisten them with some of the bacon cooking liquid afterwards.*

**TAKES 6–7 HOURS • SERVES 6**

1.3kg/3lb piece smoked bacon

1 onion, peeled and studded with 6 cloves

large bunch herbs tied together, including bay, thyme and parsley stalks

bunch small carrots (about 12), scrubbed and trimmed

1 pointed cabbage, trimmed and cut into 6 wedges

**FOR THE MUSTARD SAUCE**

150ml pot double cream

150ml/¼ pint stock from the bacon (see method)

3 tbsp English mustard

handful curly parsley leaves, chopped

**1** Heat the slow cooker if necessary. Put the bacon in the pot with the onion and herbs, then cover with hot water. Cover and cook on High for 4 hours until cooked through.

**2** Add the carrots, then cook for 1 hour.

**3** Ladle 150ml/¼ pint of the cooking liquid into a smaller pan and set aside. Add the cabbage wedges to the slow cooker pot, then continue to cook for another 30 minutes until the cabbage is tender, but not overcooked.

**4** Meanwhile, make the sauce. Pour the cream into the reserved cooking liquid and bring to the boil. Simmer for a few minutes, then whisk in the mustard and parsley. Season with salt and pepper to taste.

**5** Remove the meat from the liquid, then carve it into thick slices. Serve on a platter with the cabbage and carrots, and moisten with a trickle of the cooking liquid. Serve the sauce in a jug on the side.

---

PER SERVING 694 kcals, protein 36g, carbs 9g, fat 57g, sat fat 23g, fibre 3g, sugar 8g, salt 4.51g

# Sweet-chilli onions

*These are great spooned on to hotdogs or into burgers – just let your kids choose their favourite.*

**TAKES 3–4 HOURS • SERVES 8**

4 onions, red, white, or two of each, sliced
4 tbsp sugar
1 red chilli, deseeded and chopped
4 tbsp sweet chilli sauce
4 tbsp tomato purée
4 tbsp rice wine vinegar or cider vinegar

**1** Heat the slow cooker if necessary. Mix the onions, sugar, chilli, sweet chilli sauce and tomato purée in the slow cooker pot. Cover and cook on High for 2–3 hours, stirring occasionally until very soft and caramelised.

**2** Stir in the vinegar and cook, uncovered, for another 30 minutes until sticky. Serve warm or cold.

PER SERVING 83 kcals, protein 1g, carbs 19g, fat 2g, sat fat none, fibre 1.5g, sugar 18g, salt 0.3g

# Squash, chicken & couscous one-pot

*This superhealthy supper might seem an unusual dish for a slow cooker, but it tastes fabulous when cooked this way as all the flavours are locked in together.*

**TAKES 3 HOURS ● SERVES 4**

2 tbsp harissa paste

1 tsp each ground cumin and ground coriander

1 small butternut squash, cut into 1cm/½in chunks (no need to peel)

2 red onions, halved and cut into thin wedges

2 boneless skinless chicken breasts, cut into bite-sized chunks

2 × 400g cans tomatoes

zest and juice 2 lemons

200g/7oz cherry tomatoes, halved

140g/5oz couscous

small bunch coriander, roughly chopped

**1** Heat the slow cooker if necessary. In the slow cooker pot, mix together the harissa, spices, butternut squash and onions with 2 tablespoons water. Cover and cook on High for 1 hour until softened.

**2** Stir in the chicken and canned tomatoes. Cover and cook for 1 hour until the chicken is cooked through.

**3** Turn off the slow cooker and stir in the lemon zest and juice, cherry tomatoes, couscous and some seasoning. Cover and leave for 10 minutes until the couscous is soft. Stir through the coriander and serve.

PER SERVING 283 kcals, protein 25g, carbs 42g, fat 3g, sat fat 1g, fibre 6g, sugar 16g, salt 0.53g

# Saucy prawns

*Ditch the takeaway menu and get the kids to make this dish in your slow cooker instead.*

**TAKES 2 HOURS • SERVES 4**

3 garlic cloves, crushed

juice 2 lemons, plus wedges to squeeze over

4 tbsp low-sugar and salt ketchup

2 tbsp sweet chilli sauce

2 tbsp caster sugar

2 tbsp rice wine vinegar

200ml/7fl oz chicken stock

400g/14oz large raw peeled prawns

steamed broccoli and rice, to serve

**1** Heat the slow cooker if necessary. Mix the garlic, lemon juice, ketchup, sweet chilli sauce, sugar, vinegar and stock together in the pot. Cover and cook on High for 1 hour until the garlic is softened.

**2** Add the prawns and some seasoning, then cover and cook for 30 minutes until the prawns are pink and cooked through. Serve with steamed broccoli and rice and lemon wedges to squeeze over.

PER SERVING 127 kcals, protein 26g, carbs 4g, fat 1g, sat fat none, fibre 1g, sugar 3g, salt 2.3g

# Easy lamb tagine

*If you're out for the day and can't add the squash part way through cooking, just cut it into wedges and put it in at the start. It may be a little soft, but will still taste delicious.*

**TAKES 8½ – 9½ HOURS • SERVES 4**

2 tbsp olive oil

1 onion, finely diced

2 carrots, finely diced

500g/1lb 2oz diced leg of lamb

2 fat cloves garlic, crushed

1 tbsp ground cumin

2 tsp ground coriander

½ tsp saffron strands (or use turmeric powder if you're on a budget)

2 tsp ground cinnamon

1 tbsp clear honey

100g/4oz soft dried apricots, quartered

1 vegetable stock cube

1 small butternut squash, peeled, deseeded and diced

chopped parsley and toasted pine nuts, to garnish (optional)

couscous, to serve

**1** Heat the slow cooker if necessary. Heat the olive oil in a big frying pan and add the onion and carrots. Cook until softened. Add the diced lamb and brown all over. Stir in the garlic and all the spices, and cook for a few minutes more or until the aromas are released.

**2** Transfer everything in the pan to the slow cooker pot. Add the honey and apricots, crumble in the stock cube and pour over 400ml/14fl oz boiling water from the kettle. Cover and cook for 2 hours on Low, then stir in the squash, re-cover and cook for 6–7 hours more until the lamb and squash are tender.

**3** Season the tagine to taste. Serve with couscous and sprinkle with parsley and pine nuts, if using.

PER SERVING 413 kcals, protein 27g, carbs 27g, fat 22g, sat fat 8g, fibre 6g, sugar 22g, salt 1g

# Italian sausage stew with rosemary–garlic mash

*Don't season with salt until cooked and ready to serve, because if you salt lentils while cooking it can prevent them from softening.*

**TAKES 7–9 HOURS • SERVES 4**

8 good-quality pork sausages
2 tbsp olive oil
2 carrots, finely chopped
2 celery sticks, finely chopped
1 onion, finely chopped
2 rosemary sprigs, 1 chopped
3 garlic cloves, roughly chopped
175g/6oz dried green lentils, rinsed
400g can chopped tomatoes
400ml/14fl oz chicken or vegetable stock
1kg/2lb 4oz potatoes, cut into chunks
150ml/¼ pint milk

**1** Heat the slow cooker if necessary. Fry the sausages in 1 tablespoon of the oil in a frying pan until brown. Transfer to the slow cooker pot with the carrots, celery, onion, chopped rosemary, half the garlic and the lentils, tomatoes and stock. Cover and cook on Low for 6–8 hours until the lentils are tender and the sausages are cooked through.

**2** Keep warm while you make the mash to serve. Boil the potatoes until tender. Drain them well.

**3** Meanwhile, in another pan, heat the milk, remaining garlic and rosemary sprig until just about to boil, then turn off the heat. Sieve the hot milk over the potatoes and mash with the remaining oil, then season. Serve with the stew.

PER SERVING 616 kcals, protein 27g, carbs 67g, fat 29g, sat fat 8g, fibre 9g, sugar 12g, salt 3.91g

# Spicy African chicken stew

*This is lovely for fans of spicy food. Be wary of the Scotch bonnet chillies, though, as they're very hot!*

**TAKES 8–9 HOURS • SERVES 4**

150ml/¼ pint hot chicken stock
175g/6oz smooth peanut butter
1½ tbsp sunflower oil
1 onion, halved and thinly sliced
1½ tbsp finely chopped ginger
½ tsp cayenne (optional)
2 tsp each ground coriander and cumin
1 Scotch bonnet chilli, deseeded and chopped
1 bay leaf
½ × 400g can chopped tomatoes
800g pack chicken thighs and drumsticks, skinned
2 small sweet potatoes, cut into big chunks
1 red pepper, deseeded and cut into chunks
good handful coriander, roughly chopped
rice, to serve (optional)
lime wedges for squeezing over (optional)

**1** Heat the slow cooker if necessary. In a jug, pour the hot stock over the peanut butter and stir until dissolved. Heat the oil in a frying pan and fry the onion, ginger, cayenne, if using, ½ teaspoon black pepper, the coriander, cumin, chilli and bay leaf until the onion is softened. Tip into the slow cooker pot.

**2** Stir in the tomatoes and the peanut stock, then stir in the chicken pieces, sweet potatoes and pepper. Cover and cook on Low for 7–8 hours until the chicken is tender. Season to taste and stir in most of the chopped coriander.

**3** Serve sprinkled with the reserved coriander, with some lime wedges for squeezing over and some rice, if you like.

PER SERVING 633 kcals, protein 44g, carbs 25g, fat 40g, sat fat 10g, fibre 4g, sugar 12g, salt 0.8g

# Slow-braised pork shoulder with cider & parsnips

*Pork shoulder is the ideal cut for this warming one-pot, as it's not too fatty and not too lean.*

**TAKES 9–10 HOURS • SERVES 5**

2 tbsp olive oil
1kg/2lb 4oz pork shoulder, diced
2 onions, sliced
2 celery sticks, roughly chopped
3 parsnips, cut into chunks
2 bay leaves
1 tbsp plain flour
330ml bottle cider
450ml/ ¾ pint chicken stock
handful parsley, chopped, to garnish
mashed potato and greens, to serve
(optional)

**1** Heat the slow cooker if necessary. Heat the oil in a large frying pan and brown the meat in batches, then transfer to the slow cooker pot. Add the onions, celery, parsnips and bay leaves. Sprinkle in the flour and give it a good stir until the flour disappears.

**2** Add the cider and stock so that the meat and vegetables are covered. Season, then cover and cook for 8–9 hours on Low. Serve sprinkled with parsley, with mashed potato and greens, if you like.

PER SERVING 534 kcals, protein 46g, carbs 19g, fat 29g, sat fat 9g, fibre 8g, sugar 10g, salt 0.8g

# Pesto-chicken stew with cheesey dumplings

*If you've got a 5-litre slow cooker make the full quantity given here, but otherwise adjust the recipe according to your pot size.*

**TAKES 10 HOURS • SERVES 8**

2 tbsp olive oil

12–15 chicken thighs, skin removed, bone in

200g/7oz smoked bacon lardons or chopped bacon rashers

4 tbsp plain flour

1 large onion, chopped

4 celery sticks, chopped

3 leeks, chopped

140g/5oz each sundried tomatoes and fresh pesto

700ml/1¼ pints chicken stock

small bunch basil, shredded

200g/7oz frozen peas

**FOR THE DUMPLINGS**

140g/5oz butter

250g/9oz self-raising flour

100g/4oz Parmesan, grated

50g/2oz pine nuts

**1** Heat the slow cooker if necessary. Heat the oil in a large frying pan. Brown the chicken – you might have to do this in batches – and remove to the slow cooker pot as you go. Crisp the bacon in the pan, add to the pot, then stir in the flour.

**2** Stir in the onion, celery, leeks, sundried tomatoes, pesto and stock. Cover and cook for 8 hours on Low.

**3** Heat oven to 200C/180C fan/gas 6. Transfer to an ovenproof dish if you need to. Stir in the basil and peas, and season.

**4** For the dumplings, rub the butter into the flour until it resembles breadcrumbs. Mix in the grated cheese and add 150ml/¼ pint water, mixing with a cutlery knife until it forms a light and sticky dough. Break off walnut-sized lumps and shape into balls. Put the dumplings on top of the stew and scatter with pine nuts. Bake in the oven for 25 minutes until the dumplings are golden brown and cooked through.

PER SERVING 793 kcals, protein 42g, carbs 38g, fat 52g, sat fat 17g, fibre 5g, sugar 5g, salt 2.7g

# Lemongrass beef stew with noodles

*This is an unusual, fragrant stew. If you love Thai curries, you'll really like this.*

**TAKES 9–10 HOURS • SERVES 2**

1 tbsp chopped ginger

2 garlic cloves, chopped

3 lemongrass stalks, outer leaves removed, finely chopped

2 tbsp coriander leaves, plus extra to garnish

2 red chillies, thinly sliced (leave the seeds in if you like it spicy)

2 tbsp vegetable oil

250g/9oz stewing beef, cut into 2.5cm/1in cubes

2 tbsp dark soy sauce

1 tsp five-spice powder

1 tsp brown sugar

300ml/½ pint beef stock

100g/4oz wide rice noodles

lime wedges, to garnish

**1** Heat the slow cooker if necessary. Put the ginger, garlic, lemongrass, coriander and 1 of the chillies in a food-processor, then pulse until puréed. Heat the oil in a frying pan. Add the beef and brown on all sides. Stir in the purée for a few minutes, then scrape everything into the slow cooker pot.

**2** Add the soy, five-spice, sugar and stock. Cover and cook for 8–9 hours until the beef is tender.

**3** Just before serving, cook the noodles according to the pack instructions. Drain well, then divide between two bowls and spoon over the beef stew. Serve sprinkled with the remaining chilli and extra coriander leaves, with lime wedges for squeezing over.

---

PER SERVING 502 kcals, protein 35g, carbs 43g, fat 20g, sat fat 5g, fibre 1g, sugar 4g, salt 3.5g

# Chipotle chicken

*This smoky tomato base is also great with prawns, or break in some eggs, cook until set and serve over tortillas for a version of Huevos rancheros.*

**TAKES 7½–8½ HOURS • SERVES 4**

1 onion, chopped
1 garlic clove, sliced
2 tbsp sunflower oil
1–2 tbsp chipotle paste
400g can chopped tomatoes
1 tbsp cider vinegar
8 skinless chicken thigh fillets
small bunch coriander, chopped, to garnish
soured cream and rice, to serve

**1** Heat the slow cooker if necessary. Mix the onion, garlic, oil and chipotle paste (use 1 tablespoon for a mild flavour and 2 tablespoons for a hotter, stronger one) in the slow cooker pot. Stir in the tomatoes, cider and the chicken. Cover and cook for 7–8 hours on Low.

**2** Scatter with coriander and serve with rice and soured cream.

PER SERVING 286 kcals, protein 42g, carbs 6g, fat 11g, sat fat 3g, fibre 2g, sugar 4g, salt 0.64g

# Potato, pepper & chorizo stew with fried eggs

*This makes a lovely summer stew. If you're a vegetarian leave out the chorizo and add 2 teaspoons sweet paprika to the sauce instead.*

**TAKES 7–8 HOURS • SERVES 4**

2 tbsp olive oil

1 large onion, sliced

3 peppers (we used a mixed pack of yellow, green and red), deseeded and cut into chunks

4 garlic cloves, thinly sliced

225g/8oz chorizo, cubed

650g/1lb 7oz potatoes, cut into chunks

300ml/½ pint chicken stock

4 eggs

handful flat-leaf parsley, roughly chopped, to garnish

**1** Heat the slow cooker if necessary. Mix half the oil, the onion, peppers, garlic, chorizo, potatoes and stock in the slow cooker pot. Cover and cook for 6–7 hours on Low until the potatoes are tender.

**2** Fry the eggs in the remaining oil. Spoon the stew into bowls, then put a fried egg on top and serve sprinkled with parsley.

PER SERVING 493 kcals, protein 26g, carbs 38g, fat 25g, sat fat 8g, fibre 6g, sugar 11g, salt 1.4g

# Chicken with sweet wine & garlic

*This is a classic French dish, delicious served with buttered boiled potatoes and green vegetables.*

**TAKES 9 HOURS • SERVES 4**

2 tbsp seasoned flour
1 free-range chicken (about 1.5kg/3lb 5oz), jointed into 8 pieces
2–4 tbsp olive oil
2 shallots, finely chopped
100ml/4fl oz sweet wine, such as Sauternes
200ml/7fl oz chicken stock
sprig each parsley, thyme and bay tied with string
1 garlic bulb
50g/2oz butter
200g/7oz chestnut mushrooms
3 rounded tbsp crème fraîche
a little lemon juice, if needed

**1** Heat the slow cooker if necessary. Tip the flour into a large food bag. Add the chicken pieces, two at a time, and shake well to coat evenly. Heat 2 tablespoons of the oil in a large pan, add a few pieces of the chicken and fry on all sides until well browned – repeat in batches. Remove the chicken to your slow cooker pot.

**2** Add the shallots, wine, stock, herbs, garlic and seasoning, cover and cook for 8 hours on Low.

**3** Remove the garlic and peel the cloves. Heat half the butter and a splash of the oil in a frying pan. Add the mushrooms and fry over a moderate heat until cooked. Stir into the chicken. Wipe out the pan and add the remaining butter and another splash of the oil. Add the garlic cloves and fry gently, until lightly browned. Stir in the crème fraîche, a squeeze of lemon juice and seasoning.

**4** To serve, spoon the chicken and sauce on to a platter and scatter with the garlic.

PER SERVING 828 kcals, protein 51g, carbs 9g, fat 62g, sat fat 22g, fibre 1g, sugar 4g, salt 0.81g

# Chard, sweet potato & peanut stew

*The ground peanuts add a surprising richness and up the protein content of the stew.*
*Serve on its own in bowls, or with rice.*

**TAKES 7–8 HOURS** • **SERVES 4**

2 tbsp sunflower oil

1 large onion, chopped

1 tsp cumin seeds

400g/14oz sweet potatoes, cut into
   medium chunks

½ tsp crushed chilli flakes

400g can chopped tomatoes

140g/5oz salted roasted peanuts

250g/9oz chard, leaves and stems,
   washed and roughly chopped

**1** Heat the slow cooker if necessary. Add the oil, onion, cumin seeds, sweet potatoes, chilli flakes, tomatoes and 450ml/¾ pint water. Stir, cover and cook on Low for 5–6 hours until the sweet potatoes are just about cooked.

**2** Meanwhile, whizz the peanuts in a food processor until finely ground, but stop before you end up with peanut butter. Add them to the stew with the chard, stir and taste for seasoning. Cover and cook for another 30 minutes – 1 hour, until the chard is just cooked.

**3** Serve piping hot with plenty of freshly ground black pepper.

PER SERVING 398 kcals, protein 13g, carbs 33g, fat 25g, sat fat 4g, fibre 6g, sugar 12g, salt 0.93g

# Beef & stout stew with carrots

*Sweet slow-cooked melty carrots are one of the best bits of a rustic stew. This stew can be frozen for up to 3 months, then simply defrosted then reheated until piping hot.*

**TAKES 9–10 HOURS ● SERVES 4**

2 tbsp vegetable oil

1kg/2lb 4oz stewing beef, cut into large chunks

2 tbsp plain flour

1 onion, roughly chopped

10 carrots, cut into large chunks

400ml/14fl oz Guinness or other stout

1 beef stock cube

pinch sugar

3 bay leaves

big thyme sprig

**1** Heat the slow cooker if necessary. Heat the oil in a large frying pan and brown the meat really well in batches, then transfer to the slow cooker pot. Stir in the flour until it disappears. Add the onion, carrots and stout, and crumble in the stock cube. Season the stew with some salt and pepper and the sugar. Tuck in the herbs.

**2** Cover and cook on Low for 8–9 hours until the beef is really tender.

PER SERVING 562 kcals, protein 58g, carbs 26g, fat 23g, sat fat 8g, fibre 6g, sugar 20g, salt 1.5g

# Chinese braised pork with double spring onions

*This Chinese braise needs only jasmine rice and stir-fried pak choi to serve.*

**TAKES 8–9 HOURS • SERVES 4**

4 pieces pork osso bucco (about 850g/1lb 14oz) or pork-shoulder equivalent

1 tbsp oil

250ml/9fl oz Shaohsing rice wine or dry sherry

100g/4oz ginger, finely sliced

2 garlic cloves, sliced

12 spring onions, 8 fat ones and 4 thinner ones

1 dried red chilli (look for Kashmiri chillies for a good flavour)

350ml/12fl oz chicken or vegetable stock

1 tbsp miso paste

2 tbsp soy sauce

**1** Heat the slow cooker if necessary. Brown the pork on both sides in the oil in a frying pan, then transfer to the slow cooker pot. Deglaze the frying pan with the rice wine or sherry and add to the meat. Add the ginger and garlic. Trim the ends off the 8 fat spring onions and add these to the pot along with the chilli, stock, miso paste and soy sauce. Cover and cook for 7–8 hours on Low until the pork is tender.

**2** Chop the 4 thinner spring onions and add them to the casserole just before serving.

PER SERVING 392 kcals, protein 38g, carbs 5g, fat 21g, sat fat 7g, fibre 1g, sugar 3g, salt 2g

# Irish stew

*The trick with this classic one-pot is to use a cheap cut of meat. Middle neck or scrag end are both really flavoursome and perfect for braising.*

**TAKES 9 HOURS ● SERVES 6**

1 tbsp sunflower oil

200g/7oz smoked streaky bacon, preferably in one piece, skinned and cut into chunks

900g/2lb stewing lamb, cut into large chunks

5 medium onions, sliced

5 carrots, sliced into chunks

3 bay leaves

small bunch thyme

700ml/1¼ pints lamb stock

6 medium potatoes, cut into chunks

85g/3oz pearl barley

small knob butter

3 spring onions, finely sliced

**1** Heat the slow cooker if necessary. Heat the oil in a frying pan. Sizzle the bacon until crisp. Turn up the heat, then cook the lamb until browned. Transfer the meats to the slow cooker pot. Add the onions, carrots, herbs, stock and potatoes. Cover and cook on Low for 7 hours.

**2** Add the pearl barley and cook on High for another hour until the meat is tender.

**3** Stir in the butter, season and scatter with the spring onions. Serve scooped straight from the dish.

PER SERVING 627 kcals, protein 49g, carbs 44g, fat 30g, sat fat 14g, fibre 5g, sugar 11g, salt 2.13g

# Pumpkin, cranberry & red-onion tagine

*This vegetarian tagine is packed with flavour. Traditionally it is served with couscous, but if you've only got rice in the cupboard it'll still taste great.*

**TAKES 7–8 HOURS ● SERVES 4**

3 tbsp olive oil

2 red onions, thickly sliced

2.5cm/1in piece ginger, grated

500g/1lb 2oz pumpkin or squash, peeled, deseeded and cut into large chunks

1 tsp each ground cinnamon, coriander and cumin and harissa paste

1 tbsp clear honey

500g/1lb 2oz tomato passata

50g/2oz dried cranberries

400g can chickpeas, drained and rinsed

200g/7oz couscous

2 tsp vegetable stock granules

zest and juice 1 lemon

3 tbsp toasted flaked almonds

handful coriander, roughly chopped, to garnish

**1** Heat the slow cooker if necessary. Add 2 tablespoons of the oil, the onion, ginger, pumpkin or squash, spices, honey, passata and cranberries to the slow cooker pot. Cover and cook for 6–7 hours until the pumpkin is tender.

**2** Stir in the chickpeas and heat through for another 30 minutes.

**3** Meanwhile, tip the couscous, stock granules and lemon zest into a heatproof bowl. Pour over 300ml/½ pint boiling water, stir briefly and cover with a plate. Leave for 5 minutes. Tip in the lemon juice, almonds and remaining oil, and fluff up with a fork. Scatter the coriander over the tagine and serve with the couscous.

---

PER SERVING 449 kcals, protein 13g, carbs 67g, fat 16g, sat fat 2g, fibre 6g, sugar 23g, salt 1.93g

# Minced beef & sweet-potato stew

*You can make this with lamb mince too if you like, or even half lamb, half beef if you've got bits to use up.*

**TAKES 7–9 HOURS • SERVES 4**

1 tbsp sunflower oil

500g/1lb 2oz lean minced beef

1 large onion, chopped

1 large carrot, chopped

1 celery stick, sliced

1 tbsp each tomato purée and
    mushroom ketchup

400g can chopped tomatoes

450g/1lb sweet potatoes, peeled and
    cut into large chunks

few thyme sprigs

1 bay leaf

handful parsley, chopped

shredded and steamed Savoy cabbage,
    to serve

**1** Heat your slow cooker if necessary. Heat the oil in a large frying pan, add the beef and cook until it is browned all over.

**2** Put the mince in your slow cooker pot with the onion, carrot, celery, tomato purée, mushroom ketchup, chopped tomatoes, sweet potatoes, thyme, bay leaf and 200ml/7fl oz water. Season, cover and cook on Low for 6–8 hours until the mince and potatoes are tender.

**3** Once cooked, remove the bay leaf, stir through the chopped parsley and serve with the shredded and steamed cabbage.

PER SERVING 368 kcals, protein 29g, carbs 35g, fat 13g, sat fat 5g, fibre 6g, sugar 17g, salt 0.6g

# Chicken arrabbiata

*The name actually means 'angry' – and just like the pasta sauce, this dish is intended to pack quite a punch.*

**TAKES 8½–9½ HOURS • SERVES 6**

350ml/12fl oz red wine
3 tbsp olive oil
2 medium onions, halved and sliced
1 garlic bulb, separated into cloves
2 red chillies, deseeded and sliced
150ml/¼ pint chicken stock
600g/1lb 5oz tomatoes, finely chopped
3 tbsp tomato purée
2 tsp chopped thyme leaves
6 skinless chicken legs
chopped parsley, to garnish (optional)
pasta or mash, to serve

**1** Heat the slow cooker if necessary. Put the wine in a small pan and bring to a simmer. Let it bubble for a minute then pour it into the slow cooker pot and stir in the olive oil, onions, garlic cloves, chillies, stock, tomatoes, tomato purée and thyme with some seasoning. Add the chicken legs, pushing them under the liquid, then cover the pan and cook on Low for 8–9 hours until the chicken is tender.

**2** Serve scattered with parsley, if you like, and pasta or mash.

PER SERVING 327 kcals, protein 35g, carbs 9g, fat 13g, sat fat 3g, fibre 3g, sugar 7g, salt 0.5g

# Chicken, butter bean & pepper stew

*You can make this with chicken breasts instead, but you'll want to cook it for less time or they will dry out.*

**TAKES 8–9 HOURS ● SERVES 4**

1 tbsp olive oil

8 skinless chicken thighs

1 large onion, chopped

2 celery sticks, chopped

1 yellow and 1 red pepper, deseeded
   and diced

1 garlic clove, crushed

2 tbsp paprika

400g can chopped tomatoes

150ml/¼ pint chicken stock

2 × 400g cans butter beans, drained
   and rinsed

**1** Heat the slow cooker if necessary. Heat the oil in a large frying pan and brown the thighs on both sides. Put in the slow cooker pot with the onion, celery, peppers, garlic, paprika, tomatoes and stock. Cover and cook on Low for 7–8 hours until the chicken is really tender.

**2** Stir in the butter beans, and season well. Leave uncovered and cook for 30 minutes more to heat through.

PER SERVING 422 kcals, protein 44g, carbs 27g, fat 15g, sat fat 4g, fibre 9g, sugar 12g, salt 1.6g

# Potted ham

*If you don't have individual pots, the mix can be set in a loaf tin lined with cling film, then turned out and sliced. Perfect for entertaining, make up to a week ahead.*

**TAKES 10 HOURS PLUS CHILLING**
- **SERVES 8**

about 1kg/2lb 4oz ham hocks
10 whole black peppercorns
4 bay leaves
1 onion, 1 carrot and 1 celery stalk,
　　very roughly chopped
250g pack unsalted butter
1 bunch curly parsley, leaves picked
　　and finely chopped
small pinch ground cloves
pinch yellow mustard seeds
1 tbsp cider vinegar
rustic country bread toast, cornichons,
　　chutney or red onion marmalade,
　　to serve

**1** Heat the slow cooker if necessary. Add the ham hocks to the pot with the peppercorns, bay leaves, onion, carrot and celery. Cover with water, put the lid on and cook on High for 6 hours until the ham is tender enough to shred.

**2** Lift out the ham hocks, discard the cooking liquid and veg, and let the ham cool until cold enough to handle.

**3** Gently melt the butter in a small pan and leave it to settle. Pour the fat into a bowl, discarding the milky remains.

**4** Finely shred the ham, discarding the bones - you need 500g/1lb 2oz. Mix with the parsley, spices, vinegar, two-thirds of the clarified butter and season to taste. Divide among eight ramekins or pots. Flatten the surface, then spoon over the remaining butter and chill until the butter is solid.

**5** Serve in the pots with toast, cornichons and chutney, or dip pots in a bowl of hot water and turn out the ham onto plates.

PER SERVING 316 kcals, protein 14g, carbs 1g, fat 29g, sat fat 17g, fibre none, sugar 5g, salt 2.05g

# Chicken liver & raisin pâté

*Slow cooking makes wonderful chicken liver pâté because it allows the livers to cook so gently, but keep a close eye while cooking – it can overcook and become grainy.*

**TAKES 2 HOURS, PLUS SOAKING AND CHILLING • MAKES 4 × 100ML/ 3½FL OZ RAMEKINS**

140g/5oz chicken livers
200ml/7fl oz milk
2 shallots, thinly sliced
3 tbsp olive oil
140g/5oz butter, cut into large cubes
100ml/3½fl oz Madeira
2 medium eggs, plus 1 egg yolk
pinch grated nutmeg

**1** Soak the livers overnight in milk.
**2** Drain the livers. Heat the slow cooker if necessary. Fry the shallots in the oil and a knob of the butter until softened. Add the Madeira and bubble to reduce by half.
**3** Stir in the livers, eggs, yolk and 40g/1½oz of the remaining butter. Once the butter has melted, season and blitz in a blender until smooth. Strain into a jug; rubbing the mixture through with the back of a spoon. Discard sinewy remains.
**4** Pour the mix into four 100ml ovenproof ramekins. Sit a trivet on the base of the slow cooker – like an upturned saucer – and put the ramekins on top. Pour hot water to 1cm/½in up the side of the ramekins. Cover and cook on Low for 30 minutes–1 hour, until the mix wobbles in the middle when a ramekin is shaken gently. Chill for 4 hours, until set.
**5** Melt the remaining butter with the nutmeg then spoon this over the pâté tops. Set in the fridge.

PER RAMEKIN 480 kcals, rotein 12g, carbs 6g, fat 43g, sat fat 21g, fibre 2g, sugar 5g, salt 2g

# Sea bass & seafood Italian one-pot

*Just plonk this dish in the middle of the table, lift off the lid and your guests will realise that impressive food doesn't have to be fussy or fancy.*

**TAKES 3–4 HOURS • SERVES 4**

2 tbsp olive oil

1 fennel bulb, halved and sliced, fronds kept to garnish

2 garlic cloves, sliced

½ red chilli, deseeded and chopped

250g/9oz cleaned squid, sliced into rings

bunch basil, leaves and stalks separated, stalks tied together, leaves roughly torn

400g can chopped tomatoes

75ml/2½fl oz white wine

2 large handfuls mussels or clams

8 large raw prawns

4 sea bass fillets (about 140g/5oz each)

crusty bread, to serve

**1** Heat the slow cooker if necessary. Mix the oil, fennel, garlic, chilli, squid, basil stalks, tomatoes and wine in the slow cooker pot. Cover and cook on High for 2–3 hours until the squid and the fennel is tender.

**2** Scatter the mussels or clams and the prawns over the sauce, lay the sea bass fillets on top, cover and cook for 30–45 minutes more until the mussels or clams have opened and the fish is cooked through and flakes easily. You can keep an eye on the fish through the lid to ensure it doesn't overcook.

**3** Serve scattered with the basil leaves and fennel fronds, and eat with crusty bread.

PER SERVING 329 kcals, protein 45g, carbs 7g, fat 11g, sat fat 2g, fibre 2g, sugar 4g, salt 1g

# Chinese-braised beef with ginger

*You can't go wrong with this dish – it has such a depth of flavour. Serve it with some jasmine rice and a few stir-fried chinese greens.*

**TAKES 9–10 HOURS ● SERVES 6**

2–3 tbsp sunflower or vegetable oil
1.25kg/2lb 12oz stewing beef, cut into very large chunks
2 onions
50g/2oz piece ginger
3 garlic cloves
small bunch coriander, leaves and stalks separated
2 tsp Chinese five-spice powder
6 star anise
1 tsp black peppercorns
100g/4oz dark brown muscovado sugar
50ml/2fl oz dark soy sauce
50ml/2fl oz light soy sauce
2 tbsp tomato purée
500ml/18fl oz beef stock

**TO GARNISH**

thumb-sized chunk ginger, shredded into matchsticks
1 tbsp sunflower or vegetable oil

**1** Heat the slow cooker if necessary. Heat a little of the oil in a large frying pan. Add the beef chunks, in batches, and fry until browned then transfer the beef to the slow cooker. Roughly chop the onions, ginger, garlic and coriander stalks. Put in a food processor and whizz to a paste.

**2** Wipe any oil out of the pan in which you browned the beef. Add the paste with a splash of water and gently fry, until the paste is fragrant and softened (add more water if the paste sticks). Add to the slow cooker pot with the five-spice, star anise, peppercorns, sugar, soy sauces, tomato purée and stock. Cover and cook on Low for 8–9 hours until the beef is tender.

**3** Lift the beef out of the slow cooker and set aside. Tip the sauce into a big pan and boil until reduced by about half and thickened. Meanwhile, fry the ginger matchsticks in the oil until golden and crispy. Return the beef to the sauce and scatter with the ginger.

PER SERVING 405 kcals, protein 51g, carbs 26g, fat 11g, sat fat 4g, fibre 1g, sugar 23g, salt 3.96g

# Duck, apricot & pine nut pastilla

*This pie is worth every bit of effort. It is traditional to dust it with icing sugar.*

**TAKES 3 DAYS • SERVES 6**

6 duck legs
85g/3oz sea salt
600g/1lb 5oz goose or duck fat, melted
big bottle vegetable oil
2 onions, chopped
1 tbsp each ground cinnamon and
    ground cumin, plus pinch extra
    cinnamon for dusting
1 tsp fennel seeds
tiny pinch saffron
140g/5oz dried apricots, quartered
400ml/14fl oz chicken stock
zest 2 lemons, plus a good squeeze
    juice
50g/2oz toasted pine nuts, plus a few
    extra to garnish
4 large sheets brik or 8 large sheets
    filo pastry
1 tsp icing sugar, for dusting (optional)

**1** Rub the duck legs with the salt. Cover and chill overnight.

**2** Heat the slow cooker if necessary. Wipe off the salt and put the legs in the pot. If they don't fit, do in batches. Pour over the melted fat, topping up with vegetable oil if the duck isn't covered. Cover and cook on Low for 10–12 hours until tender.

**3** Shred the duck meat from the bone, discarding skin and bones.

**4** Fry the onions and spices until golden. Stir in the apricots, chicken stock and duck. Cook gently until moist. Add the lemon zest, juice, pine nuts and season.

**5** Heat oven to 220C/200C fan/gas 7 with a baking sheet. Brush a 22–23cm- round loose-bottomed tin with oil. Line the base and sides with half the pastry sheets. Spoon in the duck mixture. Sit the remaining pastry on top, scrunching the edges. Brush with oil. Bake for 20–30 minutes until golden. To serve, scatter with pine nuts and dust with cinnamon and the icing sugar, if using.

PER SERVING 359 kcals, protein 23g, carbs 26g, fat 19g, sat fat 3g, fibre 3g, sugar 13g, salt 0.79g

# Goan prawn & coconut curry with cumin rice

*Making an authentic-tasting curry from scratch doesn't have to take a lot of effort.*

**TAKES 4–5 HOURS • SERVES 2**

1 tbsp sunflower oil
1 onion, thinly sliced
1 tbsp grated ginger
2 garlic cloves, crushed
1 red chilli, deseeded and sliced
½ tsp each turmeric powder and chilli powder
1 tsp ground coriander
10 curry leaves
1 large potato, diced
300ml/½ pint half-fat coconut milk
8 cherry tomatoes, halved
handful baby leaf spinach
200g pack raw peeled prawns

**FOR THE CUMIN RICE**

1 tsp cumin seeds
175g/6oz basmati rice

**1** Heat the slow cooker if necessary. Heat the oil in a frying pan and fry the onion, ginger, garlic and chilli for 5 minutes until starting to soften. Scrape into the slow cooker with the spices, curry leaves, potato, coconut milk and tomatoes. Cover and cook for 3 hours on High until the potato is tender.

**2** Add the spinach and prawns. Cook for 30 minutes–1 hour more until the prawns are cooked.

**3** Meanwhile, make the rice. Tip the cumin seeds into a pan and toast over a dry heat for 30 seconds. Add the rice, salt to taste and 400ml/14fl oz water, then cover and cook for 8–10 minutes until the rice is tender and the water has been absorbed. Serve with the curry.

PER SERVING 771 kcals, protein 33g, carbs 105g, fat 22g, sat fat 13g, fibre 6g, sugar 9g, salt 0.6g

# Beef massaman curry

*Slow-cooked, meltingly tender beef, flavour-soaked spuds and a sprinkling of crunchy peanuts to finish – it's curry heaven!*

**TAKES 9–10 HOURS • SERVES 4**

400ml can coconut cream

4 tbsp massaman curry paste

600g/1lb 5oz stewing beef, cut into large chunks

450g/1lb waxy potatoes, cut into 2.5cm/1in chunks

1 onion, cut into thin wedges

4 kaffir lime leaves (available from Thai shops or dried from supermarkets)

1 cinnamon stick

1 tbsp each tamarind paste, palm or light soft brown sugar and Thai fish sauce

85g/3oz unsalted peanuts, roasted and roughly chopped

1 red chilli, deseeded and finely sliced, to garnish

steamed jasmine rice, to serve

**1** Heat the slow cooker if necessary. Heat 2 tablespoons of the coconut cream in a large frying pan. Add the curry paste and fry for 1 minute, then stir in the beef and fry until well coated and sealed. Tip into the slow cooker and stir in the rest of the coconut cream, the potatoes, onion, lime leaves, cinnamon, tamarind, sugar, fish sauce and most of the peanuts. Cover and cook for 8–9 hours on Low until the beef is really tender.

**2** Sprinkle with sliced chilli and the remaining peanuts, then serve straight from the pot with jasmine rice.

---

PER SERVING 734 kcals, protein 44g, carbs 38g, fat 46g, sat fat 21g, fibre 3g, sugar 13g, salt 1.87g

# Braised shoulder of lamb with jewelled stuffing

*You can stuff and assemble the lamb the night before, chill it overnight, then start cooking at breakfast. By the evening your dinner will be meltingly tender.*

**TAKES 12–14 HOURS • SERVES 6**

1.5kg/3lb 5oz boned shoulder of lamb
2 tbsp oil
1 onion, roughly chopped
75ml/2½fl oz white wine
350ml/12fl oz chicken stock
strip orange zest
1 cinnamon stick
2 bay leaves

**FOR THE STUFFING**

50g/2oz each stoned dates and dried
    apricots, roughly chopped
25g/1oz each dried cranberries and
    shelled pistachio nuts, chopped
handful parsley, finely chopped, plus
    extra for sprinkling
1 shallot, finely chopped
zest ½ orange
3 slices stale bread, whizzed into
    crumbs

**1** To make the stuffing, soak the dates, apricots and cranberries in boiling water for 30 minutes, then drain and squeeze dry. Mix with the rest of the stuffing ingredients and some seasoning.

**2** Unroll the lamb and season it well on both sides. Spread the stuffing over one side, then roll up the meat and secure it with string. Heat the oil in a large frying pan, add the lamb and brown it well.

**3** Heat the slow cooker if necessary. Put in the onion, wine, stock, orange zest, cinnamon and bay leaves, then sit in the lamb. Cover and cook on Low for 10–12 hours until the meat is really tender. Remove and wrap with foil.

**4** Strain the remaining juices and spoon off any surface fat, then put the juices into a wide pan and boil to reduce for 5–10 minutes, until slightly thickened. Season. Slice the lamb and serve with the sauce, and parsley sprinkled over.

PER SERVING 767 kcals, protein 50g, carbs 25g, fat 52g, sat fat 24g, fibre 2g, sugar 15g, salt 0.81g

# Mushroom, shallot & squash pie

*This pie makes a great Sunday lunch for vegetarians. If you don't need to serve six people, assemble individual pies, cook as many as you need and freeze the rest.*

**TAKES 7–9 HOURS • SERVES 6**

25g/1oz dried porcini mushrooms
600g/1lb 5oz shallots, halved
250g/9oz fresh mushrooms, sliced
1 tbsp olive oil
50g/2oz butter
50g/2oz plain flour, plus a little extra
   for dusting
2 garlic cloves, finely chopped
2 tsp finely chopped rosemary leaves
2 tsp finely chopped sage leaves
1 large butternut squash, peeled,
   deseeded and cut into chunks
250ml/9fl oz vegetable stock
500g pack puff pastry
1 egg, beaten

**1** Heat the slow cooker if necessary. Soak the dried mushrooms in 250ml/9fl oz boiling water. Meanwhile, fry the shallots and sliced mushrooms in the olive oil and butter until the shallots have softened. Stir in the flour. Scrape into the slow cooker pot and stir in the garlic and herbs.

**2** Strain the dried mushrooms over the slow cooker, stirring their soaking liquid into the shallot mixture well. Roughly chop the porcini and add to the pot too with the squash and stock. Cover and cook on Low for 5–7 hours until the squash is tender.

**3** Transfer the mixture to a pie dish.

**4** Roll out the pastry on a floured surface until big enough to cover the pie dish. Cover the pie, trimming the excess pastry. Heat oven to 200C/180C fan/gas 6, glaze the pastry with a little egg and bake for 30–40 minutes or until golden and hot through.

PER SERVING 610 kcals, protein 12g, carbs 51g, fat 42g, sat fat 21g, fibre 7g, sugar 12g, salt 1.32g

# Pot-roast pheasant with cider & bacon

*Cider and cream elevate this homely pot-roast to a dish ready to grace a dinner party.*

**TAKES 7–9 HOURS • SERVES 4**

50g/2oz butter

2 pheasants, cleaned

100g/4oz bacon lardons

1 onion, chopped

1 celery stick, chopped

4 sage sprigs, leaves chopped

2 eating apples, cored and cut into
large chunks

500ml/18fl oz cider

300ml/½ pint chicken stock

1 Savoy cabbage, finely shredded

100ml/3½fl oz double cream

mashed potato, to serve (optional)

**1** Heat the slow cooker if necessary. Melt the butter in a large frying pan. Season the pheasants, add to the pan and brown on all sides. Transfer to the slow cooker pot. Add the bacon and onion to the frying pan and cook until the onion is soft and the bacon crisp. Tip into the pot with the celery, sage, apples, cider and stock.

**2** Cover and cook on Low for 6–8 hours or until the pheasants are cooked through and tender. Turn the pheasants halfway through.

**3** Remove the birds from the dish and keep warm. Strain the remaining contents into a big pan. Tip the contents of the sieve into a serving dish. Boil the liquid until reduced by just over half, then add the cabbage, cover with a lid and cook for 3 minutes. Add the cream, check the seasoning, and continue cooking for 1 minute more. Pour over the reserved bacon-and-apple mixture, and stir together. Sit the pheasants on top and serve with mashed potato, if you like.

PER SERVING 865 kcals, protein 67g, carbs 15g, fat 56g, sat fat 26g, fibre 6g, sugar 15g, salt 1.6g

# Ginger-beer & tangerine-glazed ham

*This warming ham is great for entertaining as it's simple to prepare in advance. Many gammons don't need soaking before cooking, but check with your butcher.*

**TAKES 1 DAY, PLUS 1 HOUR TO FINISH**
**● SERVES 8**

3kg/6lb 8oz mild-cure gammon
1 onion, halved
3 tangerines, zest removed with a
    vegetable peeler, and juiced
4 star anise
2 litres/3½ pints ginger beer
small handful cloves

**FOR THE GLAZE**

3 tbsp honey
2 tbsp wholegrain mustard

**1** Heat the slow cooker if necessary. Put the gammon, onion, tangerine zest and star anise in the pot. Pour over all but 100ml/3½fl oz of the ginger beer and, if necessary, top up with water so the gammon is just covered. Cover and cook for 10 hours on Low until cooked through. Cool, cover and chill at this stage if you want to prepare ahead – bring back to room temperature before continuing.

**2** Heat oven to 220C/200C fan/gas 7. Carefully cut the skin off the gammon, making sure to leave a layer of fat, then lightly score the fat into diamond shapes. Put in a roasting tin lined with foil.

**3** Warm the honey, mustard and reserved ginger beer in a pan and boil until it thickens. Spoon over the fat, then stud a clove into the middle of each diamond. Bake for 20–25 minutes or until the glaze has caramelised. If you did prepare ahead, add another 10 minutes to the cooking time. Slice and eat warm or cold.

PER SERVING 451 kcals, protein 50g, carbs 4g, fat 27g, sat fat 10g, fibre none, sugar 4g, salt 6.49g

# Cottage chilli hotpot

*If you don't have a slow cooker with at least a 5-litre capacity you'll need to halve or reduce this recipe by a third to fit yours.*

**TAKES 10–11 HOURS • SERVES 6**

800g/1lb 12oz braising steak, cubed
2 tbsp each plain flour, seasoned well, and olive oil
300ml/½ pint red wine
2 red onions, cut into chunks
2 carrots, cut into chunks
4 garlic cloves, bashed to remove skin
2 red peppers, deseeded, cut into chunks
1 red chilli, deseeded and sliced
few thyme sprigs, plus 1 tbsp leaves
1 tsp each ground cumin and coriander
½ tsp each ground cinnamon and chilli flakes
2 × 400g cans chopped tomatoes
2 tsp caster or granulated sugar
250ml/9fl oz good-quality beef stock
400g can red kidney beans, drained and rinsed
1kg/2lb 4oz potatoes
few knobs butter

**1** Heat the slow cooker if necessary. Toss the beef in flour, then brown in a frying pan in batches with the oil and spoon into the slow cooker. Add the wine to the pan over the heat and scrape up any bits. Reduce by half, then add to the beef.

**2** Whizz the onions, carrots and garlic in a food-processor until finely chopped. Stir into the beef with the peppers, chilli, thyme sprigs, spices, tomatoes, sugar and stock. Season, then cover and cook on Low for 8–9 hours, or overnight, until the beef is tender.

**3** Stir in the beans and transfer to an ovenproof dish if you need to.

**4** Peel and slice the potatoes to 5mm thick, then boil for 5 minutes. Drain, then tip back into the pan. Add the butter and thyme leaves, season, then toss to coat. Layer the potatoes on top of the chilli.

**5** Heat oven to 200C/180C fan/gas 6 and bake for 40–50 minutes, until the potatoes are golden.

---

PER SERVING 584 kcals, protein 38g, carbs 55g, fat 23g, sat fat 8g, fibre 8g, sugar 16g, salt 1.27g

# Steamed venison & port pudding

*Serve whole for extra wow factor, then slice into the pudding in front of your guests.*

**TAKES 7–8 HOURS ● SERVES 4**

600g/1lb 5oz cubed stewing venison, such as shoulder
140g/5oz cubed belly pork, skin on
2 tbsp beef dripping or lard, plus extra for greasing
1 onion, finely sliced
1 tbsp plain flour
1 tsp thyme leaves, chopped
2 tbsp mushroom ketchup
100ml/3½fl oz port
50ml/2fl oz red wine
125ml/4fl oz good beef stock

**FOR THE PASTRY**

375g/13oz self-raising flour
140g/5oz shredded suet
1 tsp salt

**1** Mix the pastry ingredients. Add 250ml/9fl oz cold water gradually to the dough. Wrap in cling film and chill.

**2** Brown the venison and pork in batches in 1 tbsp of the dripping. Set aside. Add the remaining dripping to the pan, then the onion. Soften. Return the meat to the pan, stir in the flour, thyme, ketchup, port, wine and stock. Simmer, season and cool.

**3** To assemble, grease a 1-litre pudding basin. Roll out two-thirds of the pastry to a circle to line the basin. Add the filling, pressing it down. Roll out the remaining pastry to make a lid. Moisten the edges with water, stick on the lid and pinch to seal. Cover with a double layer of greased foil and baking parchment, folding a pleat in the sheets. Tie on with string.

**4** Sit a trivet in the base of the slow cooker – try a small upturned saucer. Sit the pudding on top and pour boiling water to halfway up the basin. Cover and cook on High for 5–6 hours, until a skewer poked in comes out piping hot.

**5** Turn out and serve.

PER SERVING 1,091 kcals, protein 47g, carbs 81g, fat 60g, sat fat 29g, fibre 5g, sugar 8g, salt 2.7g

# Thai green chicken curry

*Thai curries taste really authentic when cooked in a slow cooker, because traditionally they tend to have a thin sauce. Serve with Thai fragrant rice, if you wish.*

**TAKES 5 HOURS • SERVES 4**

300ml/½ pint coconut cream

2 tsp Thai fish sauce

1 tsp granulated palm or light muscovado sugar

4 freeze-dried kaffir lime leaves

3 boneless skinless chicken breasts, cut into bite-sized pieces

100g/4oz each mangetout and green beans, thinly sliced or halved

2 spring onions, finely shredded

lime wedges, to squeeze over

**FOR THE CURRY PASTE**

20g bunch coriander, stalks and leaves separated

2 each shallots, garlic cloves and lemongrass stalks, all finely chopped

25g/1oz fresh ginger, roughly chopped

3 small hot green chillies, finely chopped (include the seeds)

small handful basil leaves

1 tsp each ground cumin, coriander and crumbled lime leaves

1 tbsp each lime juice and sunflower oil

**1** For the curry paste, whizz the coriander stalks, three-quarters of the leaves, the shallots, garlic, lemongrass, ginger, chillies, basil, cumin, ground coriander, ¼ tsp black pepper, the lime leaves, lime juice and oil to a smooth paste. Half of this paste will serve four, chill the rest for 3 days, or freeze for a month.

**2** For the curry, heat the slow cooker if necessary. Put half the paste, coconut cream, fish sauce, sugar and lime leaves in the pot. Cover and cook on High for 2 hours. Add the chicken pieces, cover again and cook for 2 hours more on High until the chicken is cooked through.

**3** When the chicken is nearly ready to serve, steam or boil the mangetout and beans for a couple of minutes. Serve the curry in bowls with some of the veg piled on top, along with the spring onions and remaining coriander leaves. Serve with a bowl of Thai fragrant rice and lime wedges for squeezing over.

---

PER SERVING 297 kcals, protein 26g, carbs 7g, fat 19g, sat fat 14g, fibre 2g, sugar 5g, salt 0.7g

# Sustainable fish pie

*To prepare ahead, make the filling and mash, assemble, then cool and chill for up to 24 hours. To serve, heat oven to 180C/160C fan/gas 4 and bake for 30–40 minutes.*

**TAKES 5 HOURS ● SERVES 6**

400ml/14fl oz full-fat milk

50g/2oz butter, plus extra for dotting

50g/2oz plain flour

1 onion, finely chopped

2 bay leaves

good grating nutmeg

700g/1lb 9oz pollack fillet, skinned and cut into bite-sized pieces

300g/10oz raw peeled North Atlantic prawns

small bunch parsley, chopped

**FOR THE MASH**

1kg/2lb 4oz floury potatoes, peeled and chopped into chunks

50ml/2fl oz full-fat milk

25g/1oz butter

pinch freshly grated nutmeg

**1** Heat the slow cooker if necessary. Heat the milk in a pan until just about to boil. Mix the butter and flour to a paste in the slow cooker pot, then gradually whisk in the milk to a smooth sauce. Stir in the onion, bay leaves and nutmeg with some seasoning. Cover and cook on High for 3 hours, stirring every hour.

**2** Add the fish, prawns and parsley, and cook on High for 30 minutes more until the fish and prawns are just cooked.

**3** While the fish cooks, boil the potatoes until cooked, then drain well. Put the pan over the heat again, add the milk, butter and nutmeg, and mash until smooth. Season well.

**4** Heat the grill. Spoon the mash on to the fish mixture – after transferring the fish mixture to an ovenproof dish if you need to. Dot the pie with butter, then grill until golden on top.

---

PER SERVING 435 kcals, protein 36g, carbs 37g, fat 16g, sat fat 9g, fibre 3g, sugar 6g, salt 0.9g

# Slow-cooked pork belly with cider

*This recipe replicates how top restaurants cook their pork belly – slow cooking ahead of time, then simply pan-frying quickly to finish.*

**TAKES 2 DAYS • SERVES 4**

1 large carrot, roughly chopped
1 onion, roughly chopped
few celery sticks, roughly chopped
2 garlic cloves, smashed
sprig fresh thyme
2 bay leaves
500ml/18fl oz good-quality cider
small splash cider vinegar
1 litre/1¾ pints fresh chicken stock
1.2kg/2lb 12oz piece unscored
   boneless pork belly
2 tbsp sunflower oil

**1** Heat the slow cooker if necessary. Put all the ingredients except the pork and sunflower oil in the pot. Season, then slide in the pork. If it isn't submerged, top up with water. Cover and cook on Low for 6–8 hours until really tender.

**2** Once cooked, line a baking sheet with cling film. Carefully lift the pork on to the sheet. Cover the pork with cling film and cover with a flat tray or dish. Weigh the pork down with another dish and leave to cool in the fridge overnight. Strain the pot juices into a small pan, cover and chill.

**3** To serve, unwrap the pork and cut into 4 equal pieces. Lift off any fat from the braising juices, tip the rest into a saucepan and bubble down until slightly syrupy. Season to taste and keep warm.

**4** Heat the oil in a frying pan. Turn the heat down and add the pork, skin-side down – be careful as it can spit. Sizzle for 5 minutes until crisp. Flip over and cook for 3–4 minutes until hot through. Serve with the sauce and seasonal veg.

PER SERVING 915 kcals, protein 66g, carbs 10g, fat 67g, sat fat 24g, fibre 2g, sugar 8g, salt 1.22g

# Homemade pink lemonade

*Make batches of this for a garden party and your guests will be fighting for seconds!*

**TAKES 5 HOURS, PLUS CHILLING**
● **MAKES 1 LARGE JUG – SERVES 6**

8 lemons, plus extra slices to serve
200g/7oz caster sugar, plus extra
    to taste
140g/5oz raspberries, plus extra
    to serve
ice cubes, to serve

**1** Heat the slow cooker if necessary. Pare the zest from the lemons with a peeler, removing as little white pith as possible – cut away any pith you can from the strips. Juice the lemons and mix the juice, zest, sugar and raspberries in the slow cooker pot with 200ml/7fl oz water. Cover and cook for 4 hours on High.

**2** Mix the contents of the slow cooker with another litre/1¾ pints of water in a big bowl, then ladle through a sieve into another bowl or jugs. Press as much as you can through the sieve with the back of a wooden spoon. Add extra sugar to taste and chill in jugs. To serve, add a few lemon slices, raspberries and lots of ice.

PER SERVING 141 kcals, protein 1g, carbs 35g, fat none, sat fat none, fibre 1g, sugar 35g, salt none

# Elderflower, lemon & vanilla cordial

*You can keep this cordial in sterilised bottles in a cool, dark place for 2 months or in the fridge for 6 months. It you want to keep it for longer, it can be frozen.*

**TAKES 5 HOURS, PLUS COOLING**
● **MAKES 1 LITRE/1¾ PINTS**

1kg/2lb 4oz caster sugar

2 unwaxed organic lemons, halved, plus strip of peel

1 vanilla pod, split, seeds scraped out and reserved

1 tbsp citric acid powder or vitamin C powder

about 40 fresh elderflowers, shaken free of bugs and lightly rinsed

**1** Heat the slow cooker if necessary. Put the sugar, lemons, vanilla pod, citric acid or vitamin C powder and 1 litre/1¾ pints water in the pot. Cover and cook on High for 4 hours.

**2** Add the elderflowers to the pot and stir gently. Leave to cool completely, then pass through a sieve lined with muslin or a new, clean J-cloth into another clean pan. Whisk in the vanilla seeds and store the cordial in sterilised bottles with a strip of peel and the vanilla pod added.

PER SERVING (100ml/3½fl oz diluted cordial)
67 kcals, protein none, carbs 17g, fat none, sat fat none, fibre none, sugar 17g, salt none

# Mulled pear & cranberry punch

*This makes a really nice change to mulled wine – it's much fruitier and lighter and leftovers even taste good cold!*

**TAKES 2–4 HOURS • MAKES 4–5 GLASSES**

500ml/18fl oz pear cider
500ml/18fl oz pear (or cloudy apple) juice
500ml/18fl oz cranberry juice
good handful fresh or dried cranberries
75ml/2½fl oz sloe gin
1 cinnamon stick
1 vanilla pod, scored lengthways

**1** Heat the slow cooker if necessary. Put all the ingredients into the pot, then cover and cook on High for 2 hours, or Low for 4 hours.

**2** When you are ready to serve, ladle into glasses and keep the slow cooker on Low with the lid off to keep the punch warm.

PER GLASS (5) 177 kcals, protein none, carbs 27g, fat none, sat fat none, fibre none, sugar 14g, salt none

# Strawberry compote

*Delicious spooned over hot toast, panna cotta, Greek yogurt or drop scones, especially with a scoop of vanilla ice cream.*

**SERVES 4 • TAKES 3 HOURS**

500g/1lb 2oz ripe strawberries, hulled
4 tbsp caster sugar
1 tbsp lemon juice
few drops balsamic vinegar (optional)

**1** Heat the slow cooker if necessary. Cut the strawberries in half or in quarters if large, and put in the pot with the sugar and lemon juice. Cover and cook on Low for 2 hours until the strawberries have softened.

**2** Cool in the slow cooker with the lid off, then add the balsamic vinegar, if using and stir in gently.

PER SERVING 113 kcals, protein 1g, carbs 27g, fat 1g, sat fat none, fibre 2g, sugar 27g, salt none

# Easy cherry compote

*It's really worth investing in a cherry pitter to make this recipe, or you'll be stoning cherries all day!*

**MAKES 3 × 450G/1LB JARS • TAKES 4 HOURS, PLUS OVERNIGHT STANDING**

1kg/2lb 4oz cherries, stoned weight (you'll need to buy about 1.25kg/2lb 12oz, then de-stone them)
500g/1lb 2oz jam sugar (the one with pectin added)
juice ½ lemon
4 tsp brandy

**1** Mix the cherries and sugar together, cover and leave to stand overnight.
**2** Heat the slow cooker if necessary. Tip the syrupy cherries into the pot. Add the lemon juice and brandy, cover and cook on High for 2 hours, then remove the lid, give it a stir and cook, uncovered, on High for another 1 hour, stirring often.
**3** Leave the compote for 15 minutes before ladling it into sterilised jars. Keep the sealed jars in a cool, dark place for up to six months, and in the fridge for up to two weeks once opened.

PER TBSP 46 kcals, protein none, carbs 12g, fat none, sat fat none, fibre none, sugar 12g, salt none

# Apricot & orange blossom conserve

*The beauty of homemade jam is that you can make it with a lot less sugar than you'd find in bought versions.*

**MAKES 4 × 330ML JARS • TAKES 4 HOURS, PLUS OVERNIGHT STANDING**

750g/1lb 10oz apricots, halved and stoned, then diced
200g/7oz dried apricots, diced
750g/1lb 10oz preserving sugar
juice 1 lemon
1 tbsp orange blossom water
few knobs of butter (optional)

**1** Mix all the apricots and the sugar together, cover and leave to stand overnight.

**2** Heat the slow cooker if necessary. Tip the syrupy apricots into the pot. Add the lemon juice and orange blossom water, cover and cook on High for 2 hours, then remove the lid, give it a stir and cook uncovered on High for another 1½ hours, stirring often.

**3** Stir in knobs of butter, if you like – this will help to dissolve any scum. Leave the jam for 15 minutes before ladling into sterilised jars – this allows the fruit to settle so it doesn't sink to the bottom. Will keep in the fridge for 3 weeks, or freeze for up to 6 months.

PER TBSP 27 kcals, protein none, carbs 6g, fat none, sat fat none, fibre none, sugar 6g, salt none

# Cranberry jewelled mincemeat

*Nothing beats homemade mincemeat. To sterilise jars, wash them in hot soapy water,
rinse well, then leave them in a low oven to dry completely before filling.*

**MAKES 4 JARS • TAKES 9 HOURS,
PLUS OVERNIGHT SOAKING**

500g/1lb 2oz mixture of raisins,
    currants and sultanas (use jumbo or
    golden sultanas, if you can get them)
140g/5oz dried apricots, chopped
85g/3oz dried cranberries
85g/3oz mixed peel
100ml/3½fl oz brandy
zest and juice 1 lemon and 1 orange
175g/6oz suet
100g/4oz fresh or frozen cranberries,
    roughly chopped
200g/7oz soft brown sugar
1½ tsp ground cinnamon
½ tsp ground nutmeg

**1** Tip the dried fruits and mixed peel into
a large bowl. Pour over the brandy, citrus
zests and juices. Stir, then cover and
leave to soak for 24 hours.
**2** Heat the slow cooker if necessary. Tip
the fruit mixture into the slow cooker pot
with the remaining ingredients and stir
well. Cover and cook on Low for 8 hours.
Pack while hot into sterilised jars. Leave
in a cool, dark cupboard for at least a
fortnight, or for up to 6 months.

PER 2 TBSP 102 kcals, protein none, carbs 16g,
fat 3g, sat fat 2g, fibre 1g, sugar 16g, salt none

Mincemeat

# Rhubarb & ginger syllabub

*Using a slow cooker is a great way to cook rhubarb as it's nice and gentle, with no agitation, so the fruit becomes tender without collapsing into mush.*

**SERVES 4 • TAKES 3 HOURS, PLUS COOLING**

400g/14oz rhubarb, diced

thumb-sized piece ginger, peeled and finely chopped

75g/2½oz caster sugar

100ml/3½fl oz white wine

100g/4oz light mascarpone

300ml/½ pint double cream

50g/2oz icing sugar

2 pieces crystallised ginger, finely chopped

**1** Heat the slow cooker if necessary. Put the rhubarb, root ginger, sugar and white wine in the pot, cover and cook on Low for 2 hours until the rhubarb is tender. Remove from the slow cooker and set aside to cool.

**2** Whisk the mascarpone, double cream and icing sugar to soft peaks. Remove 4 tablespoons of the cooled rhubarb and mash with a fork, then fold into the cream mixture.

**3** To serve, divide the rest of the poached rhubarb between 4 glasses, reserving a bit. Spoon over the cream mixture, then top with a few pieces of crystallised ginger and the rest of the rhubarb.

PER SERVING 592 kcals, protein 5g, carbs 36g, fat 46g, sat fat 29g, fibre 1g, sugar 36g, salt 0.1g

# Steamed vanilla sponge with butterscotch sauce

*Cooking a steamed pudding on the stove ties up one of your hobs for hours and the bowl often rattles noisily. Making in your slow cooker is a much more sensible idea!*

**SERVES 4 • TAKES 5 HOURS**

175g/6oz butter, softened, plus extra
   for greasing
175g/6oz golden caster sugar
3 eggs, beaten with a fork
1 tsp vanilla extract
175g/6oz plain flour
¾ tsp baking powder
50ml/2fl oz milk
Custard or ice cream, to serve

**FOR THE BUTTERSCOTCH SAUCE**

75g/2½oz caster sugar
25g/1oz butter
50ml/2fl oz double cream

**1** Heat the slow cooker if necessary. Butter a 1-litre pudding basin. Beat the butter and sugar in a bowl until pale and fluffy. Add the eggs then the vanilla.

**2** Fold in the flour and baking powder until no lumps remain. Stir in the milk.

**3** Fill the basin with the sponge mixture and cover with a double layer of buttered foil and baking parchment, making a pleat in the centre to allow the pudding to rise. Tie the foil securely with string, then put it in the slow cooker pot on an upturned saucer. Pour in boiling water to halfway up the sides of the basin. Cover and cook on High for 4 hours until a skewer poked in comes out clean.

**4** For the sauce, dissolve the sugar with 2 tablespoons water over a low heat. Bring to the boil. Whisk in the butter when the sugar has turned into a golden caramel, then remove from the heat.

**5** When cooked, turn out the sponge onto a plate, drizzle with the sauce and serve.

PER SERVING 308 kcals, protein 18g, carbs 148g, fat 75g, sat fat 43g, fibre 2g, sugar 98g, salt 1.47g

# Blackberry, apple & pear scrumble

*Never heard of a scrumble? It's a happy accident created in the Good Food kitchen one day. We call it a 'scrumble' as we think it tastes half like a scone, half like crumble!*

**SERVES 5 • TAKES 4 HOURS**

3 Bramley apples, peeled, cored and
   roughly chopped
50g/2oz caster sugar
3 ripe pears, peeled, cored and roughly
   chopped
225g/8oz blackberries

**FOR THE SCUMBLE**

250g/9oz plain flour
125g/4½oz butter, softened
100g/4oz caster sugar
4 tbsp milk
1 tsp vanilla extract
granulated sugar, for sprinkling

**1** Heat the slow cooker if necessary. Put the apples in the pot with the sugar and 4 tablespoons water. Cover and cook on Low for 2 hours, then stir in the pears and blackberries and cook on Low for 1 hour more. Transfer to a baking dish, or 5 individual pie dishes, and chill for up to 2 days, or freeze for up to 3 months.

**2** Heat the oven to 180C/160C fan/gas 4. To make the scrumble, put the flour, butter, sugar, milk and vanilla in a food processor and pulse until it comes together in a scone-like dough. Drop clumps all over the top of the fruit, then sprinkle generously with granulated sugar. Bake for 40–45 minutes until the fruit is bubbling and the scrumble is golden and crisp. Delicious with vanilla ice cream or double cream.

PER SERVING 585 kcals, protein 6g, carbs 97g, fat 22g, sat fat 13g, fibre 6g, sugar 59g, salt 0.34g

# Syrupy plums with pistachio meringues

*This is doubly sticky – gooey, mallowy meringue, hiding under a crisp crust, is paired with syrupy plums.*

**SERVES 6 • TAKES 4½ HOURS**

1kg/2lb 4oz small plums
200g/7oz caster sugar, plus 2 tbsp
4 tbsp plum jam or quince conserve
4 egg whites
1 tbsp cornflour
1 tsp vanilla extract
25g/1oz pistachios, chopped
cream or custard, to serve

**1** Heat the slow cooker if necessary. Halve larger plums and stone them, and leave smaller ones whole. Put them into the slow cooker pot with the jam and the 2 tablespoons sugar. Cover and cook on Low for 3 hours until the plums are tender. Tip into a large, shallow baking dish. Chill until ready to finish.

**2** Heat oven to 140C/120C fan/gas 1. Whisk the egg whites in a clean mixing bowl until stiff. Whisk in the 200g/7oz sugar in 3 batches, beating the whites back to stiff between each addition. Whisk in the cornflour and vanilla and keep going until you have a lovely shiny, stiff mixture.

**3** Scoop 6 spoonfuls of the meringue on top of the plums, scatter with pistachios, then bake for 30–40 minutes until the meringues are pale and crisp on top but soft underneath. Eat warm or at room temperature, with cream or cold custard for pouring over.

PER SERVING 276 kcals, protein 4g, carbs 63g, fat 2g, sat fat none, fibre 3g, sugar 60g, salt 0.15g

# Little blueberry puddings with lemon sauce

*These little puds look deceptively sweet, but they contain a sponge bursting with berries and the sauce is deliciously tangy. Make as a treat for your loved one.*

**MAKES 2 ● TAKES 1½ HOURS**

50g/2oz softened butter, plus extra for the moulds
50g/2oz caster sugar
1 egg
50g/2oz self-raising flour
zest 1 lemon, plus 2 tbsp juice
4 tbsp blueberries
crème fraîche or Greek yogurt, to serve

**FOR THE SAUCE**

100g/4oz lemon curd
1 tsp cornflour

**1** Heat the slow cooker if necessary and put the kettle on. Butter 2 individual pudding basins or dariole moulds and line the bottoms with circles of baking parchment. Beat the butter, sugar, egg, flour and lemon zest with 1 tablespoon of the juice. Fold in the berries and divide the mixture between the moulds.

**2** Sit the moulds in the pot. Pour in boiling water from the kettle to come halfway up the sides. Bake for 1 hour on High until risen and a skewer comes out clean.

**3** Meanwhile, make the sauce. Warm the lemon curd in a small pan. Slowly mix the remaining lemon juice into the cornflour until it is a smooth paste, then stir into the lemon curd. Bubble for 1 minute, stirring, until smooth.

**4** To serve, carefully run a cutlery knife around the edge of the mould to release. Turn out onto serving dishes and spoon the lemon sauce on top. Eat with a dollop of crème fraîche or yogurt.

PER PUDDING 540 kcals, protein 7g, carbs 77g, fat 25g, sat fat 13g, fibre 1g, sugar 47g, salt 0.83g

# Apple & cornflake pots

*Kids will love these clever little pots, made with a few ingredients you should have hanging around in your storecupboard and fruit bowl.*

**SERVES 4 • TAKES 3–5 HOURS**

800g/1lb 12oz Bramley apples
3 tbsp golden caster sugar
2 tbsp golden syrup
25g/1oz butter
85g/3oz cornflakes
200ml/7fl oz low-fat crème fraîche

**1** Heat the slow cooker if necessary. Peel, core and thinly slice the apples and put in the slow cooker pot with the caster sugar and 3 tablespoons water. Cover and cook on Low for 2–4 hours until tender.

**2** Divide the mixture between 4 glass tumblers and leave to cool. Meanwhile, heat the golden syrup and butter in a large bowl in the microwave or in a small pan, for 1 minute, to melt. Add the cornflakes and stir well to coat.

**3** Top the cooled apple with the crème fraîche, then divide the cornflake mix between the glasses.

PER SERVING 372 kcals, protein 4g, carbs 60g, fat 13g, sat fat 8g, fibre 3g, sugar 44g, salt 0.8g

# Plum & amaretti semifreddo

*A ripple of sweet plum purée and chunks of amaretti biscuits turn this Italian ice cream into an all-in-one dessert – just the thing to eat outdoors when the weather is good.*

**SERVES 8 • TAKES 5 HOURS PLUS COOLING AND FREEZING**

450g/1lb ripe purple plums, halved and stoned
350g/12oz caster sugar
1 tbsp Disaronno liqueur
2 large egg whites
300ml/½ pint double cream
85g/3oz soft amaretti biscuits, roughly broken up

**1** Heat the slow cooker if necessary. Put the plums in the pot with 2 tablespoons water, 110g/4oz of the sugar and the liqueur. Cover and cook for 4 hours on Low. Allow to cool slightly, then blitz with a stick blender. Pass through a sieve to remove the plum skins. Allow to cool.

**2** Put the remaining sugar in a pan with 150ml/¼ pint water, and dissolve over a low heat. Boil for 5 minutes or until the mixture reaches 120C on a cooking thermometer. Whisk the egg whites until stiff. With the beaters running, carefully pour the sugar mixture onto the egg white, whisking until thick. In another bowl, softly whip the cream, then gently fold in the meringue mixture until smooth, followed by the slow-cooked plum pulp and biscuits.

**3** Scrape into a freezable container, cover with cling film, freeze for a few hours or until set. To serve, remove from freezer 5 minutes before scooping into balls.

PER SERVING 435 kcals, protein 3g, carbs 55g, fat 22g, sat fat 13g, fibre 2g, sugar 54g, salt 0.1g

# Classic summer pudding

*We can't think of a nicer way to celebrate all the gorgeous berries that are in season in summer than with this delicious pudding.*

**SERVES 6 • TAKES 2½ HOURS, PLUS OVERNIGHT CHILLING**

300g/10oz raspberries, plus a few extra to serve

225g/8oz blackberries, plus a few extra to serve

100g/4oz redcurrants, plus a few extra to serve

400g/14oz strawberries, hulled and quartered

140g/5oz golden caster sugar, plus a bit extra (optional)

400g brioche loaf, crusts trimmed, sliced into 1cm-thick, long slices along the wrong way of the loaf

clotted cream or single cream, to serve

**1** Heat the slow cooker if necessary. Wash the fruit then place the raspberries, blackberries and redcurrants in the pot with the sugar and 2 tablespoons water. Cover and cook for 1 hour on High.

**2** Add the strawberries, cover and cook for 1 hour. Drain the juice from the fruit, reserving both. Add sugar if necessary.

**3** Line a 1.2-litre pudding basin with a double layer of cling film. Trim one brioche slice to fit in the base of the basin. Trim other slices to the correct length to line the sides. Dip slices into the juice, then use to line the sides. Patch any gaps with remaining brioche, saving some for the base. Tip in the fruit. Finish with a brioche layer, then pour over any remaining juice. Cover with cling film.

**4** Sit a small plate on top and weigh down with two cans. Leave overnight.

**5** To serve, unwrap the film, place a serving plate over the pudding, flip it over, remove the basin and peel away the film.

PER SERVING 369 kcals, protein 7g, carbs 68g, fat 7g, sat fat 5g, fibre 6g, sugar 43g, salt 0.9g

# Boozy hot chocolate sauce

*Spoon this over ice cream in summer for a grown-up treat, or over chocolate or coffee cake in winter for a really indulgent pud.*

**SERVES 8–10 • TAKES 2 HOURS**

200g bar dark chocolate, chopped

100g/4oz butter, diced

300ml/½ pint double cream

3 tbsp caster sugar

3 tbsp Disaronno amaretto liqueur, Cointreau orange liqueur, or Tia Maria coffee liqueur – use whatever is your favourite, or in your booze cupboard

**1** Heat the slow cooker if necessary. Mix all the ingredients in the slow cooker pot. Cover and cook on Low for 2 hours, stirring briefly halfway through, then vigorously at the end.

PER SERVING (10) 377 kcals, protein 2g, carbs 16g, fat 32g, sat fat 20g, fibre 2g, sugar 15g, salt 0.2g

# Apricot & almond crumble

*You can make this with apricots, peaches or nectarines, but apricots work particularly well with almonds.*

**SERVES 6–8 • TAKES 4 HOURS**

1.5kg/3lb 5oz apricots, halved and stoned, then half diced

100g/4oz demerara sugar

100ml/3½fl oz orange juice

200g/7oz plain flour

140g/5oz almonds with skins, chopped

1 tsp ground cinnamon

200g/7oz cold butter, diced

140g/5oz caster sugar

vanilla ice cream or crème fraiche, to serve

**1** Heat the slow cooker if necessary. Mix the apricots with 40g/1½oz of the demerara sugar and the orange juice in the slow cooker pot. Cover and cook for 3 hours on Low. Scrape into a big baking dish or 6–8 individual dishes.

**2** Mix the flour, nuts and cinnamon, then rub in the butter to form crumbs. Stir in the caster sugar and remaining demerara sugar, then sprinkle over the apricot mixture. You can now cover and leave this for up to 24 hours.

**3** Heat oven to 180C/160C fan/gas 4. Bake for 40–45 minutes until the crumble is crisp and golden, then serve with ice cream or crème fraîche.

---

PER SERVING(8) 560 kcals, protein 8g, carbs 62g, fat 31g, sat fat 14g, fibre 5g, sugar 45g, salt 0.4g

# Index